The
Perfect
Plot

The
Perfect
Plot

Starting an allotment from scratch

Photography by
Kim Sayer

Foreword by
Christine Walkden

SIMON &
SCHUSTER
ILLUSTRATED

London · New York · Sydney · Toronto · New Delhi

A CBS COMPANY

First published in Great Britain in 2012
by Simon & Schuster UK Ltd
A CBS COMPANY

Text and design copyright © Simon & Schuster UK Ltd, 2012
Photography copyright © Kim Sayer, 2012

The right of Simon & Schuster to be identified as the
author of this work has been asserted by them in accordance
with sections 77 and 78 of the Copyright, Designs and
Patents Act, 1988.

1 3 5 7 9 10 8 6 4 2

SIMON & SCHUSTER ILLUSTRATED BOOKS
Simon & Schuster UK Ltd
222 Gray's Inn Road
London
WC1X 8HB

www.simonandschuster.co.uk

Simon & Schuster Australia, Sydney

Simon & Schuster India, New Delhi

A CIP catalogue record for this book is available
from the British Library

ISBN: 978-1-84983-833-7

Editorial director: Francine Lawrence
Photography: Kim Sayer
Writer: Jo Monroe
Project editor: Serena Dilnot
Designer: Sally Bond
Production manager: Katherine Thornton
Commercial director: Ami Richards

Printed and bound in China
Colour reproduction by Dot Gradations Ltd, UK

Contents

From a bare field to plots full of success…

I have cultivated the land now for over forty years and know well that growing is one of the greatest gifts and experiences we can have. But I have always said that gardening is not only about growing plants: it's about growing people as well. As gardeners we take a seed, put it into prepared earth and then spend months giving it tender loving care to ensure it grows, develops, flowers and fruits. In sharing our passion and helping each other on an allotment site, we do exactly the same with people. The beginner is entering a world of the unknown, but with support and guidance from more experienced gardeners the human 'seed' is germinated, grown on and eventually blooms.

In early September 2011 I was invited down to Cornworthy in Devon to visit some hillside allotments. The site probably has the best views of any in the UK, looking over the River Dart to Haytor and Dartmoor in one direction and to Torquay the other way.

What I saw was an allotment site in its infancy. It started two and a half years ago when the Cornworthy Allotment Association was formed with a founding committee of six people. The aim was to provide allotments for local people. The site was secured with a private agreement from a very generous and thoughtful local landowner who was keen to support the project – and what a project it is turning out to be.

One allotment holder stood out during my visit – though not in a brash and outlandish manner, for he himself was self-effacing, speaking modestly of what he does and what he has contributed. He is a mature, well-established 'plant' with much wisdom and knowledge and his name is Steve. I was told several times that he kindly leads all those who need his assistance. His nickname is 'Steve Sez': the beginners and others who share this special piece of land all listen to what Steve says and then follow his advice. In this way the 'young plants' grow in skills and confidence – though I doubt very much that Steve and some of the others are aware they are cultivating young gardeners as well as plants. And these, in turn, will cultivate others. Children and adults are all growing together on this site.

Cornworthy allotment holders have become more than just occasional visitors to their plots; they have become a friendly community, and are organised without being regimented or tied to a rulebook. This must be down to Elizabeth Sherwood, who is the Secretary of the committee and one of those people who quietly and cheerfully gets everyone to do what they are meant to do without being a bossy boots. Every committee in the land needs someone as dedicated as she is.

The site has a communal shed in which the equipment is stored and this is a meeting place for a chat. (I was touched to see that some of my old articles from 'Christine's Corner' had been put up on the walls. I hope the beginners found them helpful.) They have constructed a composting lavatory, straw-bale urinal, water-harvesting system and a solar-powered borehole and are fully sustainable. It is impressive to see what has been achieved in so short a time, by people who never thought they were interested in gardening until they had a go. Kim Sayer, the photographer who had the idea for this book, has captured the development of the allotments from a bare field to plots full of success with sensitivity and feeling. For some it's vegetables, others fruit – and one person has created a wildflower meadow of such delight that it looks like a star-filled sky at night.

Gardening not only cultivates the land, but also the mind, the body and the spirit and what I saw – in the smiling faces, the pride that they shared with me in their achievements, the sense of camaraderie and the confidence to go on and make this site a permanent feature of the village – was fantastic. On this site all sorts of people are gardening together. Gardening is a real leveller. Whatever your background, social status, political leanings, ethnic origins and experiences, everyone has to work the land in the same way, plant at the same time, cultivate the plants with the same skills and fight off the same problems. All experience the same failures and delights. On my visit I also saw people who are growing together in another way. I was told that people have found out all sorts of unexpected things about friends and neighbours they thought they already knew well. They would probably never have made these discoveries if they had not gardened together, and they felt all the richer for this experience.

I was more than pleased to be invited to look at the site as I gain so much pleasure out of seeing people learning how to grow. My life is so rich for I know that the soil is my floor, the countryside my walls and the sky my ceiling. Others who garden will come to know this with time and will see and enjoy the changing seasons, the smells that are only found on an allotment site, the successes of barrowloads of crops and the delights of sharing what they have grown with their families, for these are the rewards of growing plants.

Writing this foreword has given me considerable pleasure and pride, along with a sense of feeling flattered and honoured to have been allowed into a very special world on a Devon hillside. I wish all the people who cultivate this site over the years considerable success. For the people reading this book and looking at the lovely photographs, I hope you will be inspired to sow, grow and develop, and enjoy the many different harvests that gardening can bring.

Happy growing to you all.

Christine Walkden

A working village

Cornworthy squeezes into a small valley in the beautiful South Hams district of Devon. From a distance, the village looks like a scene on a picture postcard, with the high street zigzagging its way towards the square spire of a Norman church. But as you get closer, you realise the chocolate box packaging disguises a proper working village. Tractors make perfectly judged manoeuvres through the narrow lanes on their way from barn to field. There is a village pub, but no Olde Tea Shoppes selling Devon teas and no guest houses to encourage the summer tourists who swarm over the rest of the county.

When the children's author Ruth Manning-Sanders wrote a guide to the river Dart in the 1950s, she declared that Cornworthy 'does not appear particularly delightful: its narrow street straggles up the hill, flanked by darkish, unattractive houses'. She was clearly in a bad mood that day, but she did the village an enormous favour: the tourists largely stay away.

Cornworthy is far enough from the beautiful River Dart to be ignored by caravanners and self-caterers, and the second-homers who leave other villages feeling half-abandoned for much of the year have overlooked Cornworthy in favour of its thatched and rose-covered neighbours. Despite its glorious climate, Cornworthy is far enough inland to be untroubled by day-trippers from Torquay and Paignton. In short, Cornworthy is both unspoilt and unvarnished.

It's not surprising, then, that such a no-nonsense village has attracted so many no-nonsense residents. So when people started talking about their desire to grow their own vegetables, there was little chance that it would remain idle village chit-chat for long…

Cornworthy's 'narrow street straggles up the hill'. St Peter's Church stands on the hill overlooking the village, which is located in a valley in south Devon

The project

A journey begins with the
first step. In Cornworthy,
one person sowed the
seed of an idea – and the
search for the perfect
plot was set in motion

How it started

It began with a letter. In December 2008, Cornworthy resident Bill Petheram wrote to the parish council requesting the provision of an allotment site. The seed he sowed fell on fertile ground: the council decided to do something about it.

Bill had heard that councils have an obligation to look for a suitable site if at least six people make a written request for one. Two of the councillors – Steve Hunt and Elizabeth Sherwood – were keen gardeners and knew that other people in the village wanted to grow their own fruit and vegetables, so they set about finding out just how many villagers would like an allotment if a site could be found.

The councillors put up some posters in the village and wrote an article for the parish magazine, asking for interested people to get in touch with the parish clerk, Elizabeth Sherwood. Within ten days, Elizabeth had received nineteen letters of interest. She started researching the options.

You are lucky if you have someone like Elizabeth as a neighbour. She is, by all accounts, constantly cheerful and endlessly helpful, and within a few weeks she had become something of an expert on allotment law in England. The crucial piece of legislation is the information Bill had heard about, the Small Holdings and Allotments Act (1908), which requires councils to provide land for allotments if six residents request that they do so. The councillors started asking around to find out if any land was available and, just a few months later, a field owned by a local charity came up for rent for the first time in twenty-five years. It all seemed meant.

In order to sign a legal agreement with the charity, the allotment holders needed to become an official allotment association. Elizabeth got in touch with the South West Counties Allotments Association (SWCAA), who offered fantastic support for the fledgling association. 'It only cost £2 to join,' recalls Elizabeth, 'and they had templates for every kind of document we needed, whether it was to help

Below *Brassicas are slow-growing crops but will cover bare plots over winter if you choose the right variety*

Opposite *The first sign that the allotment project had become a reality*

us write our own constitution, or to draft a tenancy agreement. I can't praise them enough, they were incredibly helpful every step of the way.' Using an SWCAA template, Elizabeth drew up a constitution for the association. Bill Petheram, the original letter writer, agreed to become the Chairman, local resident Paul Hunt became the Treasurer and Elizabeth was the new Cornworthy Allotment Association's Secretary. The original team was completed by Steve Hunt, Site Manager; Nigel Coales, Composting Advisor; and Ginnie Pease, Growing Advisor. Everything seemed to be going so well.

Then the association learned that their bid for the tenancy of the charity field had failed: there had been a higher bidder. Elizabeth wrote to the nineteen would-be allotment holders and asked them to keep mentioning it to other people in the village: she felt sure that somebody somewhere would have a piece of land they could use.

It doesn't take long for information to reach everyone in a place like Cornworthy, and village gossip soon yielded results. Two of the potential plot holders, Ginnie Pease and Jo Pountney, were having Sunday lunch with friends and discovered that one of them had a two-acre field that he thought would be perfect. Elizabeth wondered whether it was just the kind of chat people have when they're socialising, but the next morning the landowner arrived on her doorstep, bringing with

him a copy of the site plan and his solicitor's details.

The landowner had bought the field as part of a bigger deal, without any firm ideas about how he would use it. His primary concern was to protect it from developers and he had been thinking about putting it to some conservation use, perhaps by planting a wood. He would have got a small grant from the government for this, but taking a peppercorn rent from the Allotment Association was another way of protecting the land while also helping the local community.

At this point, there was no need for the parish council to stay involved and the landowner and the Allotment Association drew up the legal agreement between themselves, amending one of the standard templates from the SWCAA to meet their needs. The field's owner made a few requests when the agreement was drawn up (he wanted to retain shooting rights over the allotments, for example), but one stipulation was that plot holders didn't have individual sheds. Since the field is in the middle of an Area of Outstanding Beauty, the plot holders thought it was sensible that they shared one big shed instead. Essentially the arrangement was straightforward and in September 2009 the Cornworthy Allotment Association signed a ten-year tenancy agreement on Upper Slade field for a rent of £150 a year, with an agreement to extend the tenancy after five years. The hard work was about to begin.

Left *In a very short time the allotments began to look as if they had been there for years*

Right *Dahlias were just a twinkle in the eye of the early plot holders but didn't take long to appear*

Setting up an allotment association

Waiting lists for allotments are now so long that many people are giving up hope of ever being able to grow their own food. The good news is that you don't have to wait for an allotment to become available: you can take action and force your local council to provide more allotments.

If six residents – they must be on the electoral roll or pay council tax – each write to their town or parish council asking for the provision of an allotment, then the council must take action. If you want to quote the relevant legislation in your letter, you should refer councillors to Section 23 of the Small Holdings and Allotments Act (1908), which states: 'If the council of any borough, urban district, or parish are of opinion that there is a demand for allotments . . . , the council shall provide a sufficient number of allotments . . .'. Section 25 of the same act also gives councils the power to make compulsory purchases of land for allotments.

To sign a legal agreement with either the local authority or a private landowner, you'll need to form yourselves into an official association. This isn't as hard as you might imagine, and there's plenty of help available. Setting up your own allotment association has many benefits: not only will you create a constitution (draft templates are easily found online) that sets out each plot holder's responsibilities so that you all know where you stand, but once you have formed your association, you are eligible for grants to help you prepare and improve your land.

- **JOIN THE NATIONAL SOCIETY OF ALLOTMENT AND LEISURE GARDENERS** (NSALG) (www.nsalg.org.uk) They have regional representatives who can advise you on the best way to set up and establish a successful association.

- **APPLY FOR GRANTS** A number of organisations make small (or sometimes slightly larger) amounts of money available to official allotment associations with proper constitutions and well-run committees, particularly if you aim to be ecologically sustainable. The Cornworthy Allotment Association received funds from both the district and county councils, as well as from the Devon Community Foundation and Devon Renaissance. These paid for their shed, borehole and solar panels, among other things. Most areas of the country have equivalent organisations that make grants to grassroots projects. The NSALG website has suggestions of organisations you can approach and your local council will know of others in your area with available funds.

- **BE ORGANISED** Establish an organising committee for your association and meet regularly in the early months to make sure everyone has their say and that progress is monitored.

You'll need a Chair, a Treasurer to handle the accounts and a Secretary to keep paperwork in order. Hold annual elections for these posts so that the burden doesn't keep falling on the same shoulders. Once your association is up and running, meeting once every three months should be all that's needed.

The Cornworthy villagers and plot holders gather for the Hartnells' annual barbecue in the Three Oaks field by the River Dart

Getting ready

Upper Slade field was in quite a state in July 2009: the previous owner had moved mature oak trees there a few years earlier, and all 220 of them had failed to take root. With so many trees in the field, ploughing had been impossible, and the weeds had taken advantage: some of the dock plants were waist high. Add the fact that the field is north-west facing and it might not seem the most inspiring place to start an allotment site from scratch.

'When you come from the village in the bottom of the valley up to the top of the hill here, and you look out at the view, you just want to get cracking,' says Steve Hunt, who calls himself a 'gardener-cum-gofer'. The beautiful River Dart runs along the bottom of the valley, stretching out towards the sea that is visible above Torquay on the coast. On a clear day, you can see right the way along Dorset's Jurassic Coast to Chesil Beach and Portland Bill. Inland, you are presented with stunning views of Haytor, a granite outcrop bursting out of the Dartmoor horizon. It's not hard to see why the view is so inspiring.

After decades working on local farms and gardens, Steve has become the site manager for the association. He has his own tractor and he looped a chain round the trees and pulled them up by driving off. That was the fun part. Chopping up the wood and taking it away took Steve a little longer.

Some people might see the next decision as controversial: in order to deal with the docks, Steve sprayed the field with glyphosate. 'I know a lot of people don't like using any kind of chemical,' he says, 'but even organic farmers use glyphosate. You can buy it in garden centres as Roundup. It's less toxic than things like coffee and alcohol. I'm not suggesting you could drink it, but I'm a hundred per cent certain it's safe to use on ground you are going to be planting veg in.'

The next step was getting the field ploughed. Cornworthy is the kind of village where people are happy to help out – particularly with a project like this – and a local farmer volunteered. Meanwhile, the land was surveyed by Elizabeth's husband Alun, who works as an architect. He drew up plans for 17 plots, each measuring 20 × 10 metres. Three of these were divided in half, creating 20 plots in all (14 full-size and 6 half plots). The plots were laid out in rows, with 3 metres between each row, and 1.5 metres between each plot within the rows.

Knowing that the field was home to hundreds, if not thousands, of rabbits, Steve suggested that they keep the plots at least 4 metres from the perimeter hedges. They couldn't stop the rabbits coming out of the hedges, but if there was a little bit of room for them to roam and munch, they might find enough food without needing to burrow into the plots. This strip also allowed room for the hedgecutter to cut the hedges that surround the site.

Although the plots are equal in size, some were seen as more desirable than others. Those at the top of the field, for example, would be closer to the shed, while those at the bottom had a better view of the river. Bill Petheram was given plot No. 1, to thank him for writing the original letter; all the other plot holders were allocated their parcel of land in a lottery, to prevent anyone's nose being put out of joint.

'Gardener-cum-gofer' Steve Hunt, always finding jobs to do, clears the last pieces of the unwanted trees

Once the individual plots had been marked out, Steve got to work on doing something that might seem really odd: he planted daffodil bulbs. He got hold of 30–40 kilos of bulbs and put them all along the hedgerow because he wanted to attract bees to the site. Most crops need pollination, but there hadn't been any flowers in the field for years. Early-flowering daffodils would send out a signal to the bees so that they would get in the habit of visiting the field. Steve also encouraged plot holders to plant flowers for cutting, for the same reason.

The owner of the land had given the Allotment Association access to the field a couple of months before the legal agreement was officially signed, which meant that all this preliminary work could be done in the summer, while the weather was still good. The committee wanted to hand over the plots to the allotment holders in the autumn, so they would have a chance to get their patch ready before winter set in. The plot holders signed their individual tenancy agreements in October, and suddenly the field that had been neglected for so long became a hive of activity as everyone tried to turn over their plot before the ground got too hard to dig.

It was at this point that Steve realised, a little late in the year, that he hadn't turfed the paths between the plots and the activity was compacting the newly ploughed earth. In hope rather than expectation, he scattered several kilos of grass seed in late October to establish the paths. Conventional wisdom says this wouldn't give the seed sufficient time to establish before winter, but the seed germinated and the paths slowly turned from brown to green. And then the frosts came, muting the colours, before the ground was finally blanketed in white. The plot holders settled down to wait for the allotments' first spring.

Above *Amy Sayer takes a break from preparing an allotment*

Left *The allotments swathed in low winter mist*

Right *Paul and Alison Henderson double dig the ground for the best results*

Winter arrives, bringing rare snow to the south Devon countryside

The bare necessities

Like all communities, the Cornworthy allotment holders needed two basics to keep them going: water and shelter. If those two could be provided, the third essential for all human societies – food – would be sure to follow.

The shed

Water, in the form of rain and a standpipe in one corner of the field, was available in sufficient if not plentiful amounts, so the committee's priority was building some shelter for the growers. With winds whipping in from the sea and across from Dartmoor, it can get pretty harsh in Upper Slade field.

The association's secretary, Elizabeth Sherwood, takes up the story: 'Because we're in an Area of Outstanding Natural Beauty, we knew we'd have difficulty with planning permission for any structures, so we came up with the idea of having a communal shed rather than lots of individual sheds. That also meant that there wouldn't be lots of foundations and concrete footings dotted all over the place, which wouldn't have been good for any future use for the field.'

From the beginning, the allotment holders wanted to be as inclusive as possible, which meant making sure all the facilities were suitable for disabled access. 'We wanted a wheelchair user to be able to come straight from their car, into the shed and get to their plot,' Elizabeth recalls. 'So when the man from the planning department told us to put the shed in the far corner of the field we told him to forget it: we said we'd get one of those metal lockable stores instead because you don't need permission for them. You should have seen his face! He promptly told us a shed at the top of the field would be fine, just so long as we lowered the height of it a bit!'

Left *Steve Hunt digs footings for the communal shed*

Right *Bella, the photographer's dog, inspects the foundations*

Elizabeth Sherwood had been applying for grants from local councils and organisations from an early stage. South Hams District Council Sustainable Community Locality Fund gave the association £150 in October 2009, and Devon County Council offered £500 in December. The shed was bought with a grant of £2,000 from the Devon Community Foundation's Grassroots fund.

Each plot holder has their own space to store tools and there are plans to use some of the money from grants and subscriptions to buy more tools for communal use, like a lawn mower. As well as being somewhere to store tools, the shed is a place where people can meet and catch up. But this isn't just about sharing gossip, it's also a way of pooling information. Shortly after the plot holders realised there was clubroot in the field, a disease which affects brassicas, someone saw an article by the TV gardener Christine Walkden, showing her readers what they could do to minimise the effects of the disease on their crops. When lots of the allotmenteers said how useful they'd found it, several more of Christine's articles found their way into the shed and on to its walls. It could be mistaken for a shrine to the famously no-nonsense gardener.

The toilets

The next project to make life easier for the allotment holders was the installation of toilet facilities. A straw-bale urinal was quickly installed, later followed by a composting toilet, which consists of a shed with a seat that has a hole in it. Beneath the hole is a pit, and once sawdust is added, the waste composts down with hardly any smell at all.

The borehole

Elizabeth secured another grant for a more ambitious project: a borehole to replace the inadequate standpipe. Local organisation Devon Renaissance had funds available to support environmental and community initiatives and awarded £6,230.66 to meet the costs of getting the borehole drilled. After putting the job out to tender, the allotment holders got ready for Drill Day.

'It was quite exciting when it happened,' remembers Elizabeth. 'We got a diviner in to look for water. I was a little sceptical, but as he doesn't charge unless he finds you water, I didn't see that there was a risk. He didn't say much when he got here. He just looked around and then got his rods out. They just looked like two bits of bent wire – I was expecting something much more hi-tech – but there were a couple of places where they started waving about. I still wasn't convinced when he started drilling the next day, especially when all that was shooting up into the air was a lot of dust from the slate that's under the soil here. I kept asking him if he was sure.' The next day, the diviner came back to carry on drilling and, once he'd got below 200 feet, the spout of dust turned into a water spout – he had tapped into an underground spring.

Initially the Association planned to use a petrol pump to raise water from the borehole to the storage tanks, but there were concerns that it wasn't environmentally friendly, and that it could be noisy. 'It was our landowner who suggested solar panels,' recalls Elizabeth, 'and there was enough money from the Devon Renaissance grant to buy them.'

The pump takes water from the borehole to two massive 1,500-litre storage tanks near the shed. There is then a gravity feed to a number of smaller tanks on the slope and at the bottom of the site, so that each allotment is only a short walk away from water. There are no hosepipes on the site, so it's a case of dipping a watering can into the tanks and carrying it to the plots. It can be tedious in dry weather, but everyone agrees that it would be irresponsible to take too much water from the spring.

And if those home comforts aren't enough, plot holder Jenny Hawkes often drives up to the site in her motorhome: as well as somewhere to sit in the warm, she's got a stove and kettle for a spot of lunch or a cup of tea. Allotment gardening has never been so civilised!

Opposite top
Ladies' long-drop loo

Opposite bottom
Gents' straw-bale loo

Above *No hosepipes are allowed, so watering cans and buckets are used*

Right *Borehole site*

Tools

When you first get an allotment, you can spend a lot of money on tools and other equipment. One of the great benefits of growing fruit and vegetables at an allotment site rather than in your own garden is that you can often share the more expensive tools that are only used occasionally with other plot holders, and share their cost too.

Most of the Cornworthy growers already had some tools at home, but the prospect of lugging them half a mile uphill from the village meant many preferred to double up and buy extra tools for their plot. Thefts from allotments are not unheard of – there has been a break-in at Cornworthy – and so no one wants to leave expensive equipment in a shed, even if it is locked whenever the site is unattended. The solution is to buy a few well-chosen tools that aren't too expensive and that will be used on virtually every visit. The list starts with two essential buys – a fork and a hoe.

- **FORK** A fork can be just as good at turning over heavy soil as a spade, and will do the job much more effectively in stony ground. Many people find a fork puts less strain on their backs than a spade, and it can also be used for lifting root crops and turning compost heaps. It's worth buying the best-quality one you can afford.

- **HOE** Everyone at Cornworthy has found that suppressing weeds is their biggest challenge, and a hoe is your best weapon for keeping on top of them. As long as you keep your hoe sharp, it simply slices off the tops of weeds and leaves them lying on the soil surface where the sun will desiccate them.

  When crops are planted in neat rows, hoeing between them is a doddle. With a long-handled (or Dutch) hoe, you don't have to bend or get down on your knees. Short-handled onion hoes can be used to weed between individual plants.

  As well as suppressing weeds, a hoe also loosens the soil particles and aerates the topmost layer of soil.

- **SPADE** A good spade will cost twice as much as the cheapest you can find, but it will last three times as long. Not all spades are called a spade – some are labelled ladies' spades. These have a smaller, shorter blade (the bit that goes into the ground) and are usually lighter. Many professional gardeners prefer them. A sharp spade can be used for edging paths and creating drills for sowing seeds in, as well as for digging.

- **SECATEURS** These are essential for trimming back plants that overgrow their station, pruning young fruit trees and bushes and harvesting cut flowers. Buy the best you can afford and get them sharpened regularly, at least once a year.

- **KNIFE** A sharp knife will allow you to harvest cucumbers, courgettes and pumpkins and take cuttings without damaging the rest of the plant. It is also handy for cutting string, getting stones out of shoes and making picnics. Invaluable.

- **TROWEL** Perfect for transplanting seedlings and bulbs. Long-handled trowels give greater leverage and many people find them easier to use.

TRUG You'll need something to put your produce in so you can carry it home. A trug or basket is ideal, but anything that lets you lie vegetables flat and transport it without squashing the contents will do.

BUCKET/TUB During summer and autumn you can guarantee that you will always be collecting weeds or cutting back unwanted growth. Putting it in a handy tub or bucket makes getting all your green waste to the compost heap much, much easier.

WATERING CAN Hosepipes are banned at Cornworthy and many other allotment sites, so a watering can is therefore vital. Anything less than a 2-gallon can and you'll be making lots of unnecessary trips back and forth to the standpipe; anything more than 3 gallons and you'll be making unnecessary stops to rest your back and arms.

Make sure your watering can has a fine rose attached to the spout when you are watering seeds or you will wash them all out of the ground.

Look after your tools properly and they will last longer and do less damage to your crops. Clean all tools after use. Sharpen knives and secateurs regularly, and give them a good squirt of WD-40 to help keep them rust free. It is also essential to disinfect them on a regular basis and particularly after pruning sick plants: this prevents diseases being passed on from one plant to another.

Feed the soil

❝ My father was a farmer and I worked for several local farmers before working my way up to be head greenkeeper on a local golf course. I also studied horticulture and agriculture for a year. I've been growing for other people for years, and I really wanted to grow things for myself. In the past I've been able to use a little bit of other people's land, but I never knew if they were going to ask to have it back. Here, with a proper tenancy, I can plant fruit trees that'll take a few years to establish because I know I'll still have the plot.

Because I'm known as the professional gardener round here, I try and help out as much as I can with advice for other people, and I try and show them how much they can get out of their plot. If you work it well, you can be eating all year round from your allotment.

After the fencing and paths went down, one of the first things I did was put in some griselinia as a windbreak. It's quite an exposed site up here, so I also put in some Jerusalem artichokes for the same reason – there's only so many of them you can eat, and the ones you can't eat make a really good screen.

The soil here isn't bad, but it really needs feeding. I dug in a load of manure when I first got the plot and I dig more in throughout the year. If you look after the soil it will look after your plants. I use fish, blood and bone when I plant out or put seeds in. Just a little bit in the hole can make a big difference, and it seems to keep feeding the plants for months. I also have a water butt to make a comfrey feed in. In July I filled a big swede net with a 50:50 mix of nettles and comfrey, which I grow on the plot, and put that inside the butt to stew for two or three weeks. The nettles provide the nitrogen and the comfrey provides the potash. It really stinks, I mean *really*, so you have to make sure no one is around when you use it, but come August when it's ready the crops really respond to a good soak with it.

I read quite a lot about gardening and one of the things I've tried in the past couple of years is planting according to the phases of the moon! I know it sounds a bit strange, but when you think that the moon can pull up billions and billions of gallons five or ten metres twice a day in the oceans, why couldn't it have the same effect on groundwater? My son buys me a book every Christmas called *In Tune With The Moon* and it sets out the lunar calendar for the whole year and it's very precise about when to plant particular crops. So far, I think it's been quite successful, but of course, what's more important is the weather. If you have a harsh winter or an early spring, that changes when you need to plant things. For instance, last year the farmer in the field over the valley planted his maize in May, but this year, in 2011, April was so hot that it went in early.

I have to say, my sweetcorn was a bit of a disaster last year and if I'd followed the farmer's lead I'd have done all right. It's all about soil temperature, so either start them off under glass or in a propagator, or wait till the soil is warm enough outside.

I stagger my planting so I don't get a glut. I'll usually leave a fortnight between rows of beans and peas. That way, you also lessen the risk that you've got your planting times wrong. I plant to avoid the carrot fly, which generally comes twice a year – first in April and then in August. I sow my carrots in May to avoid the first visit, and then put boards up to protect them from the second. Carrot fly come in close to the ground, so if you put up a barrier they tend not to find your carrots, but you can never tell till you pull them up in September and October. I put broccoli and cabbage under Enviromesh to stop butterflies laying eggs on them. I put metal spikes in the ground, make hoops out of bits of water pipe and lay the material over the top – there's no point in buying ready-made hoops because they'll always be the wrong size.

I only net raspberries as they start to ripen. If you net them all year, the birds are always wondering what's under the net, but if you wait till they ripen to net, then the birds get put off. It helped that in our first year there was a sparrowhawk and buzzard flying around, but this year the blackbirds have cottoned on to the fact there are a lot of us growing fruit up here, and they're starting to be a pest. We've had some sawfly attack our gooseberries, so I kick mine every time I come out to shake the caterpillars on to the ground where the blackbirds will see them. Hopefully it will keep them off my raspberries.

Strawberries were very successful last year. When they stopped fruiting, I pulled off the runners and a lot of the old leaves so that as much energy as possible would go back into making stronger plants for this year. Strawberry plants are usually good for three or four years. After that I'll take runners and pot them on to make plants for the following year. So far my fruit and my potatoes have given me the best yields, but I think people like it when they see I have a problem with a crop. On the plot next door, Elizabeth has done much better with her artichokes than I have with mine, and I think that gives everyone confidence. I've been doing this all my life and I still get things wrong, and some years will always be better than others. **"**

Keep on top of the weeds. 'One year's seeds, seven years' weeds' is the old saying. The difference in the size of the root system on a week-old dock and a two-week-old dock is quite amazing. When they're small, they're easy to hoe, so it's best to do it every time you come up.

Plant what you like most

❝ I didn't mean to get an allotment. I only said I would become the secretary initially because I was on the parish council and I wanted to help. But then I found that whenever I did some work for the Association I was so happy. There was just something about this project that made me want to get more and more involved. And of course, working with Steve on the committee meant I got my arm twisted. Steve is one of the most passionate gardeners you'll ever meet and he became our site manager. By the time we'd got the field, I knew I was going to have a go.

I thought I would take half a plot because at the time I was a full-time carer for my mum and my mother-in-law and I didn't think I would have the time or the energy or the skills. It was my husband Alun who persuaded me that a full plot wasn't an awful lot more effort than a half one, and now I'm very glad I've got all this space.

Steve's advice was to plant the things I liked the most, and so I keep part of my plot for growing flowers. I'd never grown vegetables before, so I felt more confident with flowers and I planted a lot of spring bulbs. Every time I came up in the spring to sow some seeds I went home with an armful of tulips. It was a really good incentive for coming up here when it was still a bit cold and windy.

I've planted a lot more in my second year because I learnt so much doing it last year – and I now grow vegetables to feed my sheep too! I started off with just four or five crops because there was so much else to do to start with, like laying the paths and doing the fencing, but after a few months I started wishing I'd planted more. I only did a couple of rows of potatoes because I was convinced I wouldn't be able to grow them, but they grew . . . and grew and grew. This year I think we'll be self-sufficient in potatoes. I'll keep them in the ground and harvest them when we need them.

My artichokes were a big success. I had twelve heads off one plant and over the winter I covered them in manure and they've come back beautifully this year. I was delighted with my onions last year, so I've planted more of those too, because they seem to like it here. I also did well with peas and pumpkins. The pumpkins really surprised me: I don't have a greenhouse so I put the seed straight in the ground in March, and as they grew I put collars made out of plastic plant pots around them to protect them from the wind. From one tiny seed I got lots of massive fruit.

There's so much to learn that you can't possibly know everything straight away and you can't possibly get the best results to start with. But you learn and you get better. It's great knowing that next year I'll get the chance to put into practice the things I've learnt this year.

I haven't yet learnt the different varieties of vegetables. I don't know what sort of pea I'm growing or what kind of onion. It doesn't matter to me, because I know I'll eventually pick all that up. You can't know everything straight away, can you? The great thing about being up here, apart from the view, of course, is that you can see what other people are doing and take ideas from them. If you see people supporting their peas, then you'll make supports. I've just learnt to puddle my leeks, and I've already shown someone else how to do it. We're all sharing and learning and it's fantastic.

We've been very lucky with pests and diseases. The slugs haven't cottoned on to the fact we're here yet. We've had no blackfly this year, just some sawfly who stripped the leaves of our gooseberries. Our big problem is weeds. Before we cleared the field it was waist-high in docks, and they just keep coming back. I've really made the effort to keep on top of them, partly because it looks so much nicer without the weeds, and partly because I don't want them choking my veg.

The second year has been much easier, all the hard work we did at the beginning has paid off. It is daunting to begin with, but it gets easier. I'm already excited about our third year and I haven't harvested half of what I've grown this year yet! 99

Elizabeth Sherwood feeds her sheep vegetables that she grows on her plot

The plot

Finding the perfect plot
is only the first part of
the story. Next comes
the hard work of clearing
and digging and planning
— and then the fun begins

Opposite top *Protective fencing was essential, to deter hungry rabbits*

Opposite bottom *Sophie and Jonty Tucker tension their fencing*

First steps

When people get an allotment plot it is often half derelict. Abandoned by the previous tenant, it is likely to be full of weeds, crowding out unidentifiable crops, so that it can be difficult to know where to start. The Cornworthy plot holders had a completely different problem: there was nothing there at all. A blank slate. Virgin territory. Nothing. It can be just as daunting to deal with all that bare earth as it is to deal with waist-high weeds. What on earth do you do first?

The initial plot holders signed their tenancy agreements in October 2009 and for most of them the priority wasn't planting: the most important thing was preparing the ground before winter made work on the site unpleasant and difficult.

The first task was fencing, because there were rabbits in the field. Each plot holder spent about £100 on stakes and chickenwire and the fences were buried about 15 centimetres under the soil.

The next task was as simple as it was hard: dig. Although the field had been ploughed, the soil needed to be broken down further to make it fine enough for seeds to germinate and take root. It also needed some improvement.

Preparing the soil

Looking across the valley at Cornworthy tells even an inexperienced gardener that the Devon soil is suitable for nurturing crops: all the way from the coast to Dartmoor, skewed rectangles of crops are artfully hemmed by hedgerows, and tractors move silently over the landscape like children's toys. This is unmistakably farming country.

However, there is no such thing as perfect soil. The Cornworthy soil is quite workable most of the time but it still needs regular additions of organic matter and fertiliser.

It's also full of stones and is prone to drying out because a) it's fairly free draining, and b) the site is windy. Without a hosepipe, getting the necessary amount of water to each plot could take several hours of ferrying a watering can back and forth. If ever there is a recipe for losing interest in your new allotment, it is hours spent tediously watering.

The only real solution is to dig in as much organic matter as possible. 'It's not just adding nutrients,' Steve Hunt explains, 'it's adding structure. The more manure, or failing that compost, you can add to your soil, the more water it will hold on to and the less watering you need to do.'

A professional gardener, Steve told everyone to add as much manure to their soil as they could get their hands on. The fact that he has his own tractor meant he was able to bring manure up to the field, and for a small contribution the plot holders could use it on their allotments. 'The truth is things will grow anywhere, on anything, but the more you can help your soil, the more you'll get out of it.'

Some allotment holders felt the ploughing had been enough and didn't dig their patch, but others thought differently.' One guy, Paul Henderson, was up here throughout the winter,' recalls Steve, 'just digging it over and over. He put in loads of manure and pulled out all the stones which he used to make his paths with, and guess what – he's won best allotment for the two years we've been here. That work he did with the soil has definitely had something to do with his success.'

Whether you start with a bare patch of earth or inherit a derelict patch, the time you spend preparing the soil may seem like hard work, but in the months and years to come, you will – quite literally – reap the benefits.

Clockwise from top left *FYM – farmyard manure; Steve Hunt calls on his tractor to move materials around the site; fresh manure needs to be left to rot down to a dark, crumbly texture before use; preparing to spread manure over a newly fenced and marked-out allotment*

Soil

Every plot, every garden, has its quirks and the secret of successful growing is to understand your soil and work with those quirks. No matter what you do, you can't change your underlying soil type, but you can improve it. By and large, there are four distinct soil types – chalk, peat, clay and sandy – and they each have their benefits and drawbacks.

- **CHALK** soils tend to be light, which means they warm up early in the spring and you can get a head start on other growers. However, they are usually free draining and prone to drying out. By the end of the season they can be exhausted as all the nutrients have been washed out.

- **PEAT** soils tend to be rich in nutrients and are very good at holding on to moisture. However, they are acidic which can stunt root growth. Brassicas are particularly unhappy on acidic soils and you'll need to add lime or a good alkaline compost, such as mushroom compost.

- **CLAY** soils are naturally fertile but tend to have drainage problems: in wet conditions they can be sticky and unworkable, and in droughts they can form brick-like clumps. The best course of action is to add as much organic matter as possible. The hours spent digging in manure will give the soil structure and improve its drainage. Particularly waterlogged areas may benefit from the addition of horticultural grit.

- **SANDY** soils are easy to dig and warm up quickly but they find it hard to hold on to water and nutrients. Sandy soils benefit more than any other soil type from the addition of organic material.

No matter what soil type you have, to grow crops you need to encourage the best possible mix of nutrients, moisture and air. Digging in manure and compost is the best way to achieve this.

The more you plant, the more loam you produce, as with each year more organic matter gets added to the soil. Established allotments sometimes have a metre of topsoil, whereas at Cornworthy it's less than a quarter of that.

Paul Henderson carefully evens out the topsoil after double digging his plot

Weather

There are plenty of reasons why south Devon is a popular tourist destination, and one of them is definitely the weather. Its southern latitude means spring arrives early, and summer frequently hangs around until well into October. Resorts like Torbay and Torquay can brag about being the English Riviera because the Gulf Stream keeps winters relatively mild, while the hills of Dartmoor shelter south Devon from the worst of the Atlantic winds. It has been estimated that the growing season in the south of England is fifty days longer than in Scotland. If you want to grow fruit and vegetables, Cornworthy's a wonderful place to do it.

Even sites as blessed as Cornworthy have their problems and idiosyncrasies. Individual towns, villages and suburbs all have their own microclimates, and understanding the prevailing weather conditions will help you grow better crops. The best crop growers always keep a close eye on the weather: have they got a couple of hours to plant out seedlings before the rains come, or should they dig their ground over early in case the frosts come?

Winds

Conditions vary from plot to plot. At the top of the hill, the plots bear the brunt of the wind coming in from the south-west; those next to the hedgerow are protected from the worst of the winds. The exposed nature of the site has meant that tall plants such as beans have suffered and plot holders are experimenting with dwarf varieties that are less exposed to wind. Tender young plants are shrouded in collars or placed in polytunnels for further protection. Many plot holders have planted windbreaks.

Aspect

Upper Slade field faces north-west which means the soil takes a little longer to warm up in the spring, but it also means the crops are spared the fiercest of the sun's rays in the height of summer. Facing north might not be ideal, especially in winter, but it means that the field gets evening sun from May to September, which lets Cornworthy's growers put in a bit of time on their plot after they've finished work.

Frosts

Being up high, the field doesn't suffer from ground frosts, which can cling to the bottom of the valley for weeks on end during winter. However, the air frosts up at the allotments can be bracing. There's a difference between a frost in winter and a frost in spring: the first is helpful, killing off bacteria in the soil and helping to break it down into a tilth, while a late frost at the end of spring can kill off tender seedlings planted out just a few weeks before.

If you're new to growing, or new to an area, it can take a few years to understand the rhythms and fluctuations of your plot, and as soon as you think you've got to know them, a freakishly wet summer or warm winter will make you think again. Steve Hunt has been caught out by the weather so often that he doesn't make planting calendars, because every year is slightly different. He reckons you learn far more about when to plant and harvest from looking at what more experienced growers are up to. For him, that means keeping an eye on the farmers. 'I just look across the valley and see what they're doing and take my cue from the professionals,' he says. 'They can't afford to make mistakes. If they start planting, it's probably time for me to start planting.'

Perched high on the hill, this bird scarer is always buzzing

Choosing your crops

Deciding what to grow should be relatively straightforward: just ask yourself what you like to eat. While that's definitely the best place to start, the Cornworthy gang have discovered there are other factors to take into consideration. Put simply, some crops are more rewarding than others.

Which fruit and vegetables are worth growing on your plot?

What do you eat?

There's no point growing food that you don't like. Plenty of allotment enthusiasts will tell you that the veg they grow tastes much better than anything they can buy in a supermarket, but it won't really matter that the spinach/broad beans/broccoli you produce are sweeter or more tender than their commercial equivalents if they are vegetables you've avoided since childhood. And if you grow vegetables you don't much care to eat, you're going to find it hard to sustain the enthusiasm required to get you to your first harvest. So take a look in your fridge. Dig out a recent shopping list. Flick through some recipe books. And make a list of the fruit and veg that whet your appetite.

Would it be easier or cheaper to buy from a shop?

However much you like eating carrots, there's a pretty good argument for not growing them because they are relatively cheap to buy and are always available in supermarkets. Conversely, several plot holders at Cornworthy have given over some space to an asparagus crop, as this is something that is usually expensive to buy and has a limited commercial season. If there's something you like to eat but cannot get hold of easily, then that's definitely something to consider planting. Immigrant communities in the UK have long used allotments to grow vegetables from home that aren't available in shops.

Does it taste better if you grow it yourself?

Supermarkets sell green beans cheaply and in abundance, but even the British-grown crops on sale in the summer don't taste anywhere near as good as the beans you grow yourself. There are some crops that just taste so much better if they are eaten within a few hours of harvesting. Strawberries and other soft fruit almost always taste sweeter if they come from your own plot, and French, runner and broad beans will always be more tender than anything that's been sitting on a shelf after being transported for miles.

Might it be more convenient to grow some crops in your garden?

Very few of the Cornworthy allotmenteers have grown herbs or salad crops (apart from tomatoes). These are the sorts of crops that you want to have to hand when you start cooking. Stepping outside your back door for a sprig of a herb or swiping some lettuce leaves for a quick salad is much more convenient than having them half a mile away at the allotment.

Which crops will you be able to grow on your plot?

Do you have enough space on your plot?

The size of your plot determines what you can grow as some crops take up a lot of room (and may also offer low yields). If you grow asparagus, you'll soon realise why it's expensive to buy: you get a small yield per square metre. High-yielding crops like carrots take up less space (which is why they cost less). Cabbages, broccoli and cauliflowers are harvested from plants that grow much bigger than many novices realise, and you need to leave a decent amount of space between rows of potatoes so you can get in and earth them up.

If you're tempted to plant crops close together, they will start competing for light and nutrients and you'll find it very difficult to get a hoe in between them to weed.

What are the conditions on your plot?

You might enjoy eating oranges, but in the UK we just don't get enough consistent warm sunshine to produce citrus fruit (unless it's under glass). We accept that our geography limits what we can grow, but there are other factors to consider, such as the microclimate, the aspect and the soil. If your site doesn't get enough sun, or enough water, you need to plant sympathetically in order to get the most out of your plot; if your crops need more water than is available you'll quickly get disappointed.

It might take a year or more to understand just how much sun each bit of your plot gets. Making sure that crops that need sunshine get the plum spots will make a big difference to your harvest. To ensure that your crops get as much sun as possible, consider planting your rows heading north–south rather than east–west, so each plant in the row gets the same amount of sun, rather than leaving some in the shade of more established plants.

You can always see what grows well by looking at what crops other allotment holders are growing successfully. At Cornworthy, brassicas – broccoli, cabbages and cauliflower – have been affected by both clubroot and caterpillar attacks. The clubroot can be helped by adding lime to the soil, and the caterpillars can be controlled by using butterfly nets – but unless you really enjoy brassicas, it might be more worthwhile to spend your time on crops that are better suited to your conditions.

What's easy to grow?

Every crop has its own effort to reward ratio. Some crops are difficult to germinate or need a lot of cosseting, while others are susceptible to pests and diseases. New allotment holders may take a few years to work out for themselves which crops are worth the effort and which aren't, but crops that new gardeners at Cornworthy have found easy include beetroot, broad beans, carrots, courgettes, French beans, kale, perpetual spinach and squash.

Do you want to grow heritage varieties of vegetable?

Just as some vegetables are easier to grow than others, so some varieties of vegetable give better results. If you're new to keeping an allotment, going for reliable varieties is likely to increase your enthusiasm to carry on. While it might be nice to grow heritage varieties that aren't commercially available, these older varieties may have disappeared from the shelves because they require more effort or give lower yields.

When looking at seed packets, plumping for F1 hybrid varieties helps ensure a better harvest. F1 seeds are bred to produce reliable, disease-resistant plants. They might not taste quite as good as some of the niche varieties, but the chances are that they will still taste far, far better than anything from a supermarket.

What are your own circumstances?

How much time do you have?

Before you put anything in the ground, think carefully about how much time you will be able to spend on your plot, as some crops require more attention than others. Fruit trees, for instance, tend to need little maintenance, and potatoes can be left alone from planting to harvesting (although you will get a better harvest if you earth them up). On the other hand, lettuces need constant harvesting and protection from slugs. If you know you will only be able to get to your allotment once a fortnight, you will do better to choose low-maintenance crops.

When are you going on holiday?

If you know when you're going to be away, you might like to take this into account when planning what to plant. There's little point planting Brussels sprouts and parsnips for your Christmas lunch if you're planning to spend December abroad.

Do you have access to a greenhouse?

The advantage of being able to grow under glass is that you can start planting sooner and carry on harvesting for longer. Some crops – such as tomatoes and peppers – are almost impossible to germinate without a greenhouse, but you can always buy plug plants for these. When you first start, you'll probably find that coping with the demands of your plot takes enough time without spending extra hours – and months either end of the season – in a greenhouse.

How much should you plant?

How much do you need?

How many cabbages can you eat in a month before you start to hate the sight, smell and taste of cabbage? There's no point growing more than you can eat – especially when your neighbours also have an allotment and will have their own gluts to deal with.

Successional sowing – which means planting small amounts every few weeks to extend the length of your harvest – can help reduce unnecessary gluts, and good storage and imaginative cooking can make the most of your bounty. But the best way to ensure you have enough of what you want is to plant the right amount in the first place. If you have a large family, you might get through several pounds of potatoes a week; if you're on your own, you need to plant accordingly. Try and estimate how much of any particular crop you can cope with before you sow your seed.

Can you store your crops?

Some vegetables – such as potatoes and onions – can be stored for the best part of a year, and many Cornworthy growers are trying to be self-sufficient in both those crops. Potatoes can be stored in the ground until the frosts come, but they need to be lifted before winter. If you have several sacks of potatoes and onions, then you need space to store them. Cool, dark, dry space. Unless you have a suitable garage or cupboard, you might want to think twice before you plant too many. Summer crops – such as beans and soft fruit – can store well if they're frozen, but unless you have room for a big freezer, you'll have difficulty making the most of your harvest.

Overleaf A mixed bag of
vegetables fresh from the ground

Right Cabbages need
plenty of space to grow

Planning your plot

The plots at Cornworthy are 20 x 10 metres (200 square metres), though some have been divided in half as people didn't think they'd have the time to look after a full plot. Traditionally, allotments are measured in 'rods' (an old land measurement that equates to about 5 metres) and are about 250 square metres in size, but many allotments end up being a similar size to the Cornworthy plots. While it might not be quite enough land to keep a large family fed for a year, with careful planning a dedicated and skilled gardener can produce something from a plot that size every day throughout the year.

Right *Plot divided into quarters with central area of grass (see page 66)*

Below right *Ginnie Pease (left) and Jo Pountney planting fruit trees. Ginnie is a professional gardener, and Jo a dentist, and they were founder members of the allotment group. They have a very small garden of their own but love the idea of growing their own food*

Below *Dividing up a plot into sections for different plants, shrubs and trees, leaving a proportion of it to grass*

Laying out the plot

DIVIDING UP THE PLOT Steve has some advice for novices on the best way to lay out their plots. He suggests dividing them into four, making it easier to visualise each quarter filled with plants. Suddenly one big plot becomes four manageable plots and is much less daunting for most people.

INCLUDING SOME GRASS The next suggestion makes things even simpler: give one of those quarters over to grass. Now there is 25 per cent less area to think about, which frees up time and energy for the rest of the plot. Of course, that grass area isn't lost for good: it will still be available when the plot holders need the space and have the time to cultivate it, but in the meantime, the grass is suppressing weeds, keeping the soil warm and holding on to water. An area of grass has another benefit: it's somewhere for the kids to play.

Over half the plots of Cornworthy have some grass as part of their design, and it's somewhere to take a breather during a hard session with the weeds.

MAKING A CORNER FOR THE CHILDREN If you have children, think about giving them their own piece of the plot to look after. Gardening with children isn't the easiest option, but many of the Cornworthy parents have found that they have really taken to gardening once they have a patch to call their own.

KEEPING A SPACE FOR PERMANENT CROPS Many popular fruit and vegetables need to stay in the same place year after year. Fruit trees are the most obvious example of a permanent crop: no one is going to move their orchard each spring! Soft fruits such as strawberries, blueberries and raspberries benefit from remaining undisturbed in one place. Vegetables which take time to establish, such as asparagus, also need a dedicated spot on your plot. Asparagus needs a minimum area of 1.2 × 4 metres and takes up to three years to establish (depending on the age of the crowns when planted), but can be productive for twenty years.

Siting permanent structures

Planting crops in the right place can make a big difference to your plot's productivity, and an unproductive shady spot or patch of stony ground is the ideal place to site your sheds, water butts and compost heaps. Before you sketch out a planting plan, here are some of the other things the Cornworthy growers have considered.

BARRIERS A perimeter fence is useful to keep out larger pests such as rabbits, but a chain-link fence won't offer much protection from the wind. If you are on an exposed site, consider planting a barrier that can act as a windbreak or offer shade from the sun. Hardy evergreen shrubs can do the job, but so can edible options like fruit trees, sunflowers and Jerusalem artichokes.

PATHS Before you cover every last centimetre of your plot with crops, think about how you will tend and harvest them. Paths within your plot make it much easier to hoe the beds without treading on the soil and compacting it. In winter, you'll be pleased you planted crops like Brussels sprouts and leeks next to your paths so you can harvest them easily. Any paths you make should use recyclable materials. Someone else will be taking over the plot from you in due course, and you need to leave it as you find it, without the addition of heavy paving stones or unsightly builders' rubble. Some people sow their paths with grass seed, or simply leave the soil bare: it can be trodden down for a firm surface, but may become muddy in wet weather. Another option is to lay a weedproof membrane over the path and add a layer of bark or woodchips: first edge the path with gravel boards, to stop the bark spreading on to your beds.

RAISED BEDS These have become very popular recently. The sides of raised beds are built up using boards and they are then filled with topsoil. The advantages are that the soil warms up slightly earlier in the spring and the beds have better drainage. Raised beds help keep muddy boots off nicely aerated beds, because there is no need to walk on them, and there is also some evidence that they are a less inviting for slugs and snails. However, after a while it can be awkward to add more manure or earth up potatoes, as the soil level gets higher, and weeding can be difficult if the beds are too wide.

STORAGE AND SHELTER Do you need a lockable shed or store for your tools and other materials if you're keeping them at the site? A shed will also give you somewhere to shelter from the rain.

WATER Where will you be getting your water? If your plot is a long way from a standpipe or storage butt, consider getting a water carrier that enables you to transport gallons at a time rather than pints. Or you could leave space for your own water butt (assuming you have a shed roof from which to collect rainwater).

COMPOST New gardeners are amazed at how much green waste a vegetable plot creates: for every head of cauliflower you home, there is an awful lot of foliage you leave at the plot. If your allotments don't have a communal compost heap, you will definitely want to start one of your own. In fact, you'll probably need room for two, so that you add to one while using the compost from the other.

You can also buy compost bins, or make your own from a plastic dustbin: cut out the bottom, stand it upside down and cover it with the lid. You will have a neat, contained compost corner that is easily managed, and the plastic helps to warm the compost. Make sure you weigh the lid down with some bricks to prevent it flying away.

You can make your own liquid fertiliser by soaking a large cloth bag of comfrey and nettles in a water butt for a fortnight. The resulting liquid smells horrible, but will help you get more out of the land in the long run.

Clockwise from top left *Stones dug out of the soil make firm pathways; a post-and-wire system for supporting raspberry canes; collecting rainwater from the shed roof; a raised bed*

Planning the planting

KEEPING NOTES Before you start sowing, try to sketch out a map of your plot, allocating places to each crop you want to grow. Make sure you leave enough space for each crop, bearing in mind how far apart the plants need to be and how big they grow. Consider how long each crop will be in the ground, as you may be able to grow a crop of a later vegetable once the first one has been harvested. If you are using the crop rotation method, it helps to divide the plot into several separate areas, allocating one group of vegetables to each space.

Make a note of what you have planted where and the date you sowed the seeds. This will help you know when to expect to harvest, and if you do this several years in a row, you will discover which planting times lead to the most bountiful harvests. It's a good idea to mark the ends of the rows with sticks and labels. Seedlings can be very difficult to identify, and of course an empty patch of bare earth looks identical to a bare patch that's got a row of seeds hidden from view!

KNOWING WHEN TO SOW Experienced gardeners learn that there are two kinds of climate – the one above ground and the one below. The air temperature might be pleasant, but if the ground temperature is cold, seeds just won't germinate. As a general rule, most plants will start growing when the soil temperature is above 6 degrees Celsius, but when the temperature gets into the 20s, most plants will start to exhibit signs of stress and need additional watering. And odd as it might sound, some seeds – such as lettuce and rocket – will fail to germinate when it's hot as they rely on a cold spell to trigger them into life.

There's plenty of information about sowing times and spacing on seed packets, but always ask someone more experienced if you are not sure.

SUCCESSIONAL SOWING New growers are frequently encouraged to stagger their planting, sowing small amounts of each vegetable at first, and then making further sowings throughout the season

as each one starts to grow. This helps avoid gluts, but there is a further benefit to this: by spreading out your planting times you reduce the effect of the weather on your yield. You might lose some early seedlings to a harsh frost or a strong wind, but you won't lose them all.

DOUBLE CROPPING Aim to stagger your planting so that crops mature over a longer period. It is also possible to grow more than one crop in a particular space each year. When your early broad beans finish in June, for example, you can plant winter squashes or brassicas in the same spot.

Experienced growers also intercrop, which means planting quick-growing veg such as lettuces and radishes between rows of slower growers such as sweetcorn: by the time the corn gets tall enough to block out the light, the salad crops have already been harvested.

Above *Very early planting, in November, to get the plots up and running*

Opposite *The weeds-only section of the compost heap overflows as the summer growth accelerates*

Overleaf *Jenny Hawkes' allotment plan (her garden is on page 61, top)*

Short
White and
Yellow
Daffodils

AUTUMN
RASPBERRIES

QUINCE

blueberry
bushes

White

Narcissi

strawberry
x 3
POTS

2 x Rows
of Strawberries

ASTERS

PATH

GRASS

small
parsnips

PATH

White

Narcissi

ONIONS
(white)

GARLIC

SHALLOTS

LETTUCE

PATH

PARSLEY

ONIONS

PATH

Che
Tree

White Narcissi

BEETROOT

2 x Rows BROAD BEANS

ROCKE

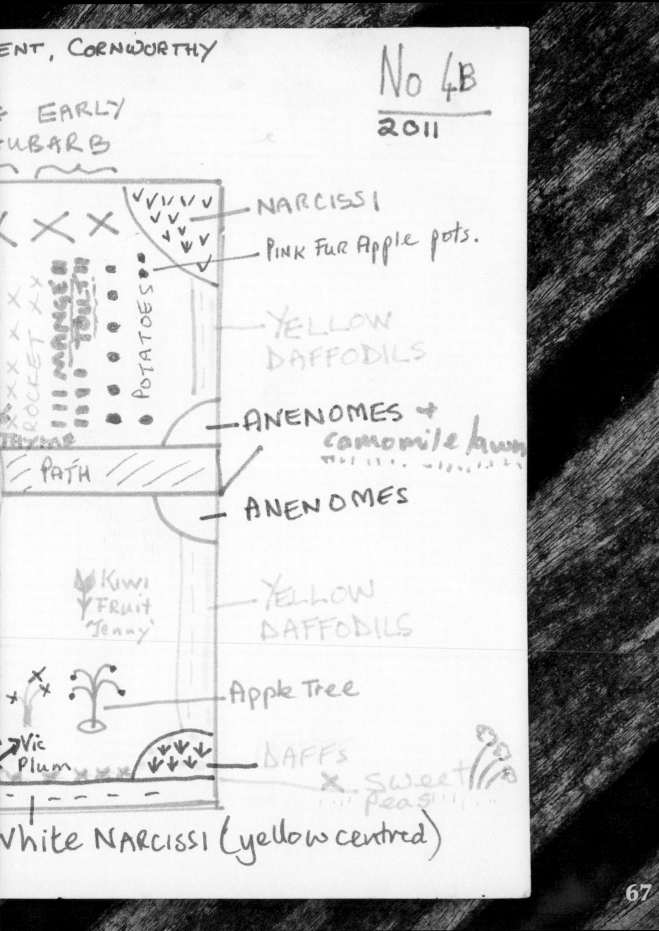

EARLY
~UBARB

NARCISSI

PINK FUR Apple pots.

YELLOW DAFFODILS

ANENOMES + camomile lawn

PATH

ANENOMES

KIWI FRUIT 'Jenny'

YELLOW DAFFODILS

Apple Tree

Vic Plum

DAFFS

sweet peas

White NARCISSI (yellow centred)

MANGEL TURLIP

POTATOES

ROCKET

Thyme

Crop rotation

It is perfectly possible to scatter a packet of seeds on unprepared beds and find yourself with something to harvest three or four months later: despite what your knees and your back might think, nature does the hardest part of the work. But the more you help nature, and work with nature, the better your harvests will be. One of the ways you can do this is by planting different groups of crops in different parts of the plot each year. This is known as crop rotation and has benefits for both you and your crops.

The theory behind crop rotation is simple: if you continue to grow the same crops in the same place each year, they will deplete the nutrients in the soil and encourage a build-up of pests and diseases. By moving certain types of crop each year, you improve the soil and grow stronger crops.

Crops are usually divided into three groups when planning crop rotation:

ROOTS (for example potatoes, carrots, parsnips)
BRASSICAS (including broccoli, cauliflower, cabbage)
LEGUMES (peas and beans)

The crops in each of these groups need the same nutrients and tend to be affected by the same pests and diseases.

Over many generations, gardeners noticed that when brassicas were grown in the same place in which legumes had been grown the previous year, the brassicas did better. This is because legumes add

nitrogen to the soil and brassicas respond well to increased nitrogen levels. You'll get better harvests if legumes are followed by brassicas, which should in turn be followed by root crops.

Growing these crops in groups can also make them easier to look after. For instance, peas and beans both need support, and cabbages and broccoli both benefit from being netted.

The more beds you have, the easier it is to rotate your crops. It is ideal to have four zones within a plot, in addition to the area where perennial crops (such as soft fruit and asparagus) are grown: one zone each for brassicas, legumes and roots, with the fourth zone left fallow (or put under green manure) or used for salad crops and squashes. If you don't have room for four beds, salads and squashes can be grown with any of the three main groups.

The trick with crop rotation is to keep a note of what you planted in which zone in which year. By making sure that you don't plant the same crop in the same bed in successive years, you will ensure the vitality of your plot for years to come.

Clockwise from top left
Ideal crop rotation: legumes (runner beans) should be followed by brassicas (kale), then by roots (potatoes) in the third year. Plant up with green manure or leave fallow for year four

The effort to reward ratio

Any gardener who has found an overlooked potato from last year pushing up new leaves through this year's neat rows of lettuces knows that, left to its own devices, nature will grow whatever it can, wherever it can. If you want to take things easy, it is perfectly possible to be a lazy and happy grower.

Although many plot holders like the idea of being as self-sufficient as possible, the reality of eating year round from your plot means starting things off early under glass, intercropping to maximise harvests and learning to store and preserve your produce. It is a lot of effort, and it takes a lot of time. Most growers will still visit a supermarket fairly often and the odd failed crop is not a matter of malnutrition or starvation as it might have been for our forefathers. If your harvest fails to materialise, the shops can always come to the rescue.

For some growers, the rewards of their labour aren't measured by the size of their harvest: the sheer enjoyment of being outside, of working with nature and learning a new skill is what motivates them, while for others getting out of the house and socialising is the prime reason for a visit to their allotment. Or it could be that the benefit comes from peace and solitude and a couple of hours switching off from work and family. What all that means is that every grower needs to calculate their own effort to reward ratio.

The plots at Cornworthy are the perfect illustration of how each grower has done this: some rectangles are meticulously weeded, fed and watered, some are cosseted under polytunnels during the cold months. Some plot holders cover their brassicas with nets to shield them from predators and protect bean shoots with mousetraps. None of this happens on other plots, and yet they all produce satisfying harvests.

Walking round Upper Slade field, it is easy to

Opposite, clockwise from top left *Steve Hunt with dibber and broad beans; Elizabeth Sherwood proudly shows off her beetroot; onions drying; Alison Henderson smiles through the effort of digging*

see which plots get the most attention, and Steve Hunt's is one of them. He puts in a lot of effort, and it shows. He digs in manure every chance he gets, he makes his own comfrey feed, he spends two hours a week with a hoe in his hand and as soon as one crop is spent he'll bring up its replacement from his greenhouse. He nets his soft fruit, has planted windbreaks and rotates his crops. This means that his sweetcorn is taller than his neighbours', his strawberries are more plentiful and his brassicas have fewer holes in their leaves. There's no doubt that Steve's plot is among the most productive at Cornworthy, partly thanks to his knowledge and skill, but also to the amount of time and effort he puts in.

Just down the hill from Steve's plot is 'delinquents' row', where many of the plot holders have not had the time to make the most of their patches. And although weeds are the most successful crop, each rectangle still produces punnet after punnet of soft fruit, trugfuls of beans and enough potatoes for a year of Sunday roasts. While the delinquents might be a little embarrassed about the state of their plots, they are more than happy with the size of their harvests. It's not as bountiful as Steve's, but then they don't expect it to be.

Some plot holders have gone to the effort of netting their brassicas and soft fruit, others have accepted that they may lose a percentage of their crop to pests: less effort may mean lower harvests, but that's a compromise they are happy with.

A few of the allotmenteers have kept detailed records of planting plans, varieties used and planting times. Over the years, this will help them choose the varieties that suit the conditions and plant them out at just the right time. Others, however, are more than happy to sow whatever seed was available on the day they went to the garden centre.

The important thing to realise about the effort to reward ratio is that there isn't a correct formula: it's a balance that every grower finds for themselves.

John Sharland digs out stubborn weeds, while Steve Hunt (foreground) rakes over an allotment

Easy does it

" People forget that the stuff you buy in supermarkets is the Class A stuff. If you've only ever seen vegetables in a shop you might have unrealistic expectations of what your crop will look like. One of the reasons I wanted to get an allotment is because you've got the space to lose some of your crops and still have enough left over to take home. Because the seeds are cheap and I've got the space, I haven't netted my brassicas. I think you have to find a balance between effort, cost and reward. I could spend the money on nets and the time on putting them up and taking them down every time I want to weed, or I could just accept that I'm probably going to lose some of them to the cabbage white. And that not all my cauliflowers are going to look like the ones in the supermarket.

There are some things it makes sense to grow at home – fast-croppers like lettuce that you want to eat as soon as you've picked them – and some things it makes sense to do up here, either because they take up a lot of space, or because they take a long time to crop. I've been growing crops in my garden for a while but it doesn't get enough sun. I brought a cherry tree from home that hadn't produced a single cherry in three years, but up here it's thriving – and keeping the birds well fed!

In the first year I drew a plan of what should be planted where. Plans are great as long as you don't lose the piece of paper, so I can't say how closely I've stuck to it, but just sitting down and working out what you want to eat and planning to avoid a glut at certain times of year was a helpful process. Keeping a diary would also be a good idea, as would better labelling, and maybe when I retire next year I'll have the time to do all that properly. For instance, I can't remember what variety of sweetcorn I've planted, so if I like them I won't know what seed to look for next year, or if I don't like them what seed to avoid!

I find coming up here very therapeutic, and it's also good exercise and fresh air. I have a stressful job dealing with offenders, but by the time I've dug over half a yard, my brain's been somewhere else and I've had a few hours off. There's definitely a Tardis effect: I tell my wife Jane I'll be out for a couple of hours, and four hours later I'm still here. The other evening I was up here on my own, the sun was still strong, the river was beautiful, the birds were in full song: you could just sit here and look at the view and it would be worthwhile. And then there's the cycle of life stuff to contemplate: planting seed, watching it grow, harvesting it and, if you want, you can save seed and do it again the following year.

It's also very sociable. If Paul Henderson, in the next plot, and I are up here at the same time, we'll sometimes put on the radio and listen to the football, but if other people come up we turn it off. I think it's that kind of respect for other people that means the atmosphere is always friendly. It just feels good to be up here. "

No matter what size plot you get, only cultivate what you can handle. Put the rest of it under grass or use a green manure, and if you're new to growing, start with really simple crops like onions and potatoes before trying the more esoteric stuff or worrying about soil acidity and crop rotation.

Don't feel guilty about thinning out seedlings. Throwing seedlings on the compost seemed really wrong at first, but you've got to give the other ones space to grow.

PLOT HOLDER'S TALES: Sophie Tucker

Make a plan

"One of our neighbours asked if we were interested in taking a plot and I jumped at the chance. Some friends had let me use the corner of their field to grow some crops in but they had just asked if they could have their land back, so the timing was perfect for me. I knew Elizabeth beforehand, and I knew Steve to say hello to, and a couple of other people in our street have taken a plot, but there are still quite a few people I've only got to know through the allotments.

As well as the social side of things, and the appeal of growing fresh, tasty veg, I had another motivation for having a plot. I teach science to GSCE students and one of the subjects I cover is Environmental and Land-based Studies. I thought I'd be able to teach it much more effectively if I had hands-on experience.

Just after we heard that the Association had found a field, we went on holiday to Portugal and instead of lying on the beach, I got a stick and started marking out where I could plant everything! It was good fun and actually really useful, because if I made a mistake I could just kick it over and start again. My intention was to grow the things we eat the most and cook with a lot, but I was so keen to get something in the ground that first autumn that I planted some broad beans, and I hate broad beans! But I knew that in the spring I wanted something to come up early.

In our first year our most successful crop was definitely stones. In the first couple of months we pulled out bucketfuls, trugfuls, wheebarrowfuls of stones, but in the spring, there they were again. They just keep coming up. I think the worms here must have incredible muscles.

At first I thought I had taken on too much so I tried to reduce the amount of work by putting some of it under grass, giving some of it over to fruit trees and wide paths. But in the second year it's felt like I've not had enough space. I really want an asparagus bed, so the lawn will have to go. Having said that, I need to scale my ambition to fit the hours I can put in. I went up the other day and could have cried: two weeks previously I cleared all the weeds, and in a fortnight they had all come back.

There's something about the site that means you want to go up there, even though you're going to have to deal with the weeds when you get there. I recently found out that my grandfather was a market gardener, and I'm wondering if it's in the blood – I just love being outdoors and getting mucky. "

Allow yourself
enough time. I
reckon it takes two
hours just to weed
the whole plot – and
that's if I can avoid
gazing out to sea or
stopping for a chat.

Winter
wonderland

In the chill of winter, the air is crisp and clear and cleansing. Frosts harden the ground and there is nothing to do but enjoy the cycle of the seasons and wait for the first stirrings of spring

What to do in winter

For many gardeners, winter is a chance to take a break from their plots. The cycle of nature places a burden on their time in certain seasons, so when nature goes to sleep, it's a welcome opportunity to put their feet up.

There is undeniably less to do in winter, but should you find your green fingers itching with idleness, there are still some tasks you can attend to, and they will help you reap a better harvest the following year. Of course, growers with access to a greenhouse will find themselves with more to do than those who must wait for spring before they can start sowing and planting.

Early winter

HARVESTING Winter vegetables such as Brussels sprouts, cabbages and leeks are still growing, and you will need to make regular visits to your patch to continue harvesting. The flavour of Brussels sprouts improves with a touch of frost, and kale can be harvested throughout the winter, even when it is frozen. If you have been storing root crops in the ground, make sure you lift them before the frosts come.

PLANTING There are some crops that benefit from being in the ground before the snows come. You can plant shallots throughout the winter, and traditionally garlic gives the best yields when it's planted before Christmas. November and December are good months for planting bare-rooted fruit trees.

IMPROVING THE SOIL The important task of improving the soil by digging in manure should already have been done in the autumn (on heavy soils) or left until early spring (for sandy soils). The soil is usually too wet and/or cold to dig in winter and will only become compacted if it is dug in these conditions.

However, you can use this quiet time to test the acidity of your soil. A simple kit from a garden centre can tell you if your acidity has changed. If the soil has become acidic, take the opportunity to add lime. For quantities, follow the instructions on the packet. (If you do add lime, do not add organic material until late winter as adding the two together can produce ammonia; then avoid planting for as long as possible.)

If puddles are forming on your plot after rain, you need to improve the drainage in these areas. This might mean digging grit into these problem areas, or you could add some extra manure in early spring to improve the soil structure. Always avoid digging when the soil is wet or waterlogged, as this will cause compaction.

TIDYING UP Use the extra time on your hands to repair any broken boundary fences and paths. Disinfect water butts and clean and sharpen tools. Clean all containers and pots, in preparation for planting in the spring.

PROTECTING CROPS If you live in a cold area, permanent crops such as squashes and asparagus may need protection from frost. Cover the crowns with a dry mulch of straw, or use horticultural fleece. Old net curtains will do just as well, if you don't mind how they look!

Above *Steve Hunt sowing broad beans*

Left *Check boundary fences, repair any gaps and firm in loose poles*

Right *The pattern of an allotment begins to take shape*

Late winter

ORDERING SEEDS Once the ground has got too hard to dig, you can retreat indoors and start planning your next harvest. Now's the perfect time to sit down with seed catalogues and order varieties you want to try. At Cornworthy, the plot holders buy a lot of their seeds communally. Have a look at your planting diary (if you kept one) and see if you want to alter your planting schedule. Sketch out what you will plant where in the coming year.

WARMING THE GROUND In January and February, start to warm the ground by erecting polytunnels. This will make it easier to get your fork into the ground and let you start sowing earlier. You can make your own polytunnels with hoops of hose covered in plastic sheeting. If that's too elaborate,

simply spread black plastic sheeting on the soil; this will also have the benefit of suppressing weeds.

SOWING AND PLANTING When the days start to lengthen, you can sow leeks and lettuces in the greenhouse. In sheltered areas, you can also start to sow carrots and spinach outdoors, and plant out Jerusalem artichokes. Continue planting out garlic and shallots.

Above left and right
Spinach sown outdoors; and warming the ground to enable early seed planting

Right *Ginnie and Jo staking fruit trees to hold them steady in strong winds*

Left *Garlic planted in autumn will have a head start as spring begins*

Below left *Bella leads the way from the village to the allotments*

Below *Elizabeth Sherwood prepares to plant out some daffodils*

Right *Snowdrops provide bright blooms on dark winter days*

Under glass

Spring starts earlier for some growers than others, even when they live in the same village. February and March tend to be busier months for plot holders with greenhouses than for those without them.

There is something wonderful about being inside a greenhouse in the dead of winter. It enables you to enjoy being in your garden throughout the year: even on the coldest days, stepping inside a greenhouse where the winds are banished and the temperatures stay above freezing (most years) is a pleasant experience. Add to that the fact that most greenhouse gardening is done standing up rather than bending over, and it's easy to see why many greenhouse owners would never give them up.

For vegetable growers, the main advantage of raising plants under glass is that it extends the growing season from early spring to late autumn (for ornamental growers, it is often about propagation and sheltering tender plants). If your greenhouse gives you a head start of three or four weeks, you can germinate seeds earlier and stagger successional sowings more easily. You can also keep growing crops for longer at the other end of the season.

A greenhouse removes some of the risks of gardening. Instead of wondering if it's too early to sow seeds or worrying that you may not have seen the last of the frosts, a greenhouse lets you start your growing year with confidence. Seeds can be germinated in perfect conditions and allowed to become seedlings without the threat of slugs, rabbits or mice nibbling on them.

Greenhouse growing isn't without problems, however. Even in winter, plants need ventilation, and that may mean daily visits to the greenhouse to open and close windows. In summer temperatures can get so high that plants become scorched and the advice from Cornworthy is that panes should be painted or shades installed to prevent this happening.

Crucially, greenhouse plants need a lot of water, as the higher temperatures and lack of access to groundwater mean soil dries out quickly. Having a water source close to your greenhouse (a water butt to collect rainfall is the easiest and cheapest way to do this) makes this job less tiresome.

And, of course, by making the conditions ideal for seeds and seedlings, you also make them more pleasant for some of their predators: insects and fungi breed more easily under glass.

By creating Mediterranean temperatures, it is possible to grow crops such as peaches, nectarines, melons and grapes, while other fruits like tomatoes and cucumbers also thrive in the warmer conditions. The general view is that the opportunity to grow a wider range of crops outweighs the problems of greenhouse growing for most gardeners.

The majority of the Cornworthy growers have a greenhouse, lean-to or conservatory where they can start sowing their crops, but it is important to remember that seedlings are at their most vulnerable when they are transferred outside, into the soil, from their cosy, sunny shelter. Greenhouse plants are spoilt and inexperienced: they've had everything given to them without having to struggle and when they get out in the real world they're

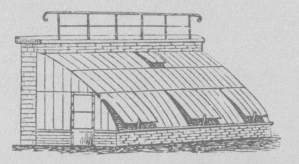

not tough enough to handle the conditions. Taking even the strongest seedlings straight from the greenhouse to the field can kill them, particularly given the high winds in Upper Slade field.

One solution to this is to gradually reduce the temperature inside the greenhouse by increasing ventilation during the day, but the best way is to harden them off in cold frames, where the seedlings can be exposed to outside conditions during the day, but protected at night from the cold spring air. Once they're ready to be transferred up to the allotment they will still need protection from the wind. It is easy to make collars from plastic plant pots or bottles: cut off the bottom and then partially bury the collar around the seedling when planting it out. The collar can be removed as the plant grows, or it can be left in place as an added barrier against slugs and mice.

There is no doubt that being able to raise plants under glass is a massive advantage to the serious grower, but many a greenhouse is bought by an enthusiastic first timer only to become a place to store bicycles and old tools within a couple of years. In the south of England, the growing season is long enough to satisfy most amateur growers, many of whom are very grateful for the respite winter offers.

Instead of buying a greenhouse when you first start growing, the advice from Cornworthy would be to wait and see how much time you have and how big your harvests are before making the commitment: many find that looking after the plot itself takes up enough of their time.

Think really carefully about where you sow your winter crops. Imagine you're going to your plot on a wet, cold and muddy day and you soon realise that the place for your sprouts and parsnips is right next to your paths! You don't want to be traipsing through the mud if you don't have to.

Anyone can do it

66 We came up here on Christmas Day last year to pick our sprouts. It was wonderful sitting down for dinner and realising that we'd grown most of our meal. If you've never eaten a sprout within two hours of it being picked then you really don't know what they taste like. They were delicious.

I come up here probably about three times a week, even in winter. I only come up here when I feel like it, and if I only do half an hour or an hour, that's OK. I want this to be a pleasure, not a chore. Last year I entered the garden competition so I felt I had to keep on top of things a bit more. This year it's been a bit more laid-back.

I'm usually here when most people are at work, so it's often just me and Kimble the dog and it's just so peaceful up here. Which was why I was shocked, and upset, when we had a break-in at the shed. It was odd what they took: an old wooden table that was only good enough for an allotment shed, some plastic watering cans, a plastic chair and a plastic wheelbarrow. They left all the tools behind! We all felt so angry because they just came in and took what they wanted. It's the only bad thing to happen since we started. Everything else about the allotments has been wonderful.

I absolutely love going home with a full basket. It's just a fantastic feeling; it's the Good Life, isn't it? In the spring it was mostly flowers, and I'd take handfuls and handfuls of daffodils and tulips but the rest of the year it's fruit and veg, even – as I say – on Christmas Day. And I'm not much of a gardener. It's all fairly new to me, but with a bit of trial and error anyone can do it. Of course, being up here if there's something I don't know how to do I just ask Steve.

In our first year, I had no idea how big some plants were going to get so I didn't leave them enough space, so things have definitely been more productive in the second season, but then that's because we're all learning. This year I think I'm going to store things properly. I lost some stuff last winter. Some of my potatoes rotted because they must have still been a bit wet when I put them away. I've also made a bit more space for them in the garage because I know how much room they take up now. Until you've harvested a lot of potatoes, how can you know how many potatoes you'll get from each plant? The other thing I'll make sure I do is to mark my parsnips properly. The tops die down in the autumn but you can leave the roots in the ground – but without the leaves, I didn't know where they were! When I eventually found them they were giants, but they still tasted great. 99

If you're trying to set up your own allotments, just persevere. When we lost out on our first field it seemed like we would never get anything. But then this became available – and we only found it because we kept talking about it.

Perseverance pays

" Because I was the one who wrote the letter to the parish council asking for the allotment site, I was allocated plot No. 1. It's right by the shed, which is handy, but it's also between the urinal and the ladies' loo, so everyone has a good look at my plot. Considering that this was all my idea in the first place, the state of my plot is really quite an embarrassment, but I've not been able to spend nearly enough time up here over the last two years. This isn't my first time growing vegetables so I know that some years you just have to be philosophical about it. Allotments are all about doing what you can when you can. For me, these first couple of years have been spent getting used to the soil and the conditions.

My plot is at the top of the field where the soil is a bit thin because the strong winds whip over the top and blow it down the hill. That's why one corner of my plot looks absolutely terrible. I've got a big pile of manure under black plastic sheets, but by next year it will have completely rotted down and I'll be able to dig it in and improve the soil. By then I'll have got rid of more stones, and in a few years' time this will be very productive. Because this field was ignored for so many years, we've had a real problem with docks. They were clearly very happy here and they keep coming back, but there are fewer this year and with perseverance we'll slowly get them under control.

One thing I made sure I found time for last year was putting in my apple trees. I planted them as cordons, and as they grow I think they will look wonderful and won't take up too much space. As expected, I didn't get a harvest from them in the first year, but this year they're looking quite bountiful. I've also put in raspberries and strawberries, and I'm experimenting with a red gooseberry. I remember gooseberries from school being sour, but these are supposed to be sweet. I won't find out till next year. Planting fruit trees is all part of taking a long-term view about this. In the second year, I made two raised beds for salad crops. One of the things I never understood about gardening is why you spend so much time digging the ground only to walk all over it! With the beds, the ground I prepare won't get compacted. Considering how little time I've been up here, I got a pretty good harvest last year. There were plenty of potatoes and garlic, and as you can never get every last potato out of the ground, quite a few have grown again this year, so that's a harvest for virtually no effort.

To be honest, the best thing has been the social side. It's just been so fantastic to see the village come together to make this happen. I had my own ideas about who would want a plot and who would be good at growing things, but my assumptions were wrong and it's been great to be surprised by who's always up here and who's getting the results. I've got to know a whole different side to my neighbours, and people are so relaxed up here that I always have really nice chats with people and find out what they've been up to. "

Spring into action

Nothing can beat the excitement of spring. Bright green buds burst forth on the trees and sturdy shoots push their way bravely out of the soil and into the air. The promise of new life is all around

Daffodils in early spring

What to do in spring

Spring is the busiest time of year in the allotment, but you will be amply rewarded later in the year for every extra hour you can put in now. There are still some winter crops to harvest in early spring, but once they're finished and cleared away, many plots are empty rectangles of brown earth. Don't worry: as new shoots start poking their noses through the soil, you'll know that all the effort was worthwhile.

Early spring

HARVESTING If winter has been kind, you will still be harvesting leeks, winter cabbage and Brussels sprouts.

PREPARING BEDS When the soil is dry and the ground is warm enough to dig, get your spade out and dig in as much organic material as you can lay your hands on (if you didn't do this in the autumn) and then rake the surface to a fine tilth. The more organic matter you add now, the less compacted and waterlogged the soil will get later in the year. Alternatively, you can mulch the plot with a layer of organic matter. This will start to raise the soil temperature while also adding vital nutrients without having to dig it in.

If you haven't done so earlier, cover the prepared ground with cloches and polytunnels and leave it for a few weeks, as this will help with warming the ground.

SOWING IN THE GREENHOUSE Open the seed packets you ordered over winter and sow trays of aubergines, peppers, sweetcorn and tomatoes. Continue sowing lettuces and leeks. If you haven't got a greenhouse, put the seed trays in an old vegetable rack in good light or on a tray on a sunny windowsill.

SOWING OUTDOORS Some crops, such as early Brussels sprouts, cauliflowers, kale, lettuces, radishes, spring onions and turnips can now be sown in drills directly in the soil. This is also the time to start sowing some broad beans and peas. Continue sowing carrots and spinach.

If you've got the time, dig trenches for your beans and peas: dig out a trench that is deeper than a normal trench (at least 30 centimetres), line it with manure or compost (you can also use fresh peelings as these will decompose in the soil), backfill the soil and sow on top.

At Cornworthy, mice have been known to dig up peas and beans as soon as they start to shoot, so plot holders give the plants some extra protection by putting plastic collars round each plant. And some leave out mousetraps.

PLANTING OUT Onion sets and seed potatoes for first earlies can go straight into the ground in early spring, as can asparagus crowns, globe and Jerusalem artichokes, perennial herbs and some varieties of strawberry. Continue planting garlic and shallots. Give every plant a handful of fish, blood and bone at the time of planting. This is a slow-release fertiliser and will keep the plants going until maturity.

Opposite, clockwise from left Young lettuces; bamboo structure for climbing plants; rows of vegetables, starting to take shape; young runner bean looking for support

Left Ground neatly prepared for sowing seed in drills

FEEDING Give crops that have been in all winter a good feed. Soft fruit bushes will like a high-potash fertiliser and all fruit trees and plants will enjoy a good mulch with organic matter, such as manure or compost.

Plants need a balance of nitrogen, potassium and phosphorus. Too much nitrogen in a liquid feed will give plenty of foliar growth but not many flowers and fruit. Potassium (or potash) helps form flowers and fruit, and phosphorus strengthens root systems.

The best approach for beginners is to dig manure and compost into the soil, add a bit of fish, blood and bone when planting and perhaps use a high-potash liquid feed for fruiting plants, including tomatoes.

Below left *Seeds, just planted and watered, begin their journey*

Below *Sprouting spring onions show winter is over*

Right *Allotmenteers Amoria and Brock Horning, with their father Jonathan, planting chitted potatoes in trenches*

103

Late spring

HARVESTING Asparagus, globe artichokes, spring cabbages, carrots, leeks, spinach, spring onions and salad crops will start to be ready now, together with some varieties of rhubarb. Hopefully, you'll always be leaving your plot with something tasty in your trug.

SOWING OUTDOORS Finish sowing Brussels sprouts and start sowing summer and winter cabbages and cauliflowers, parsnips, swedes, turnips and maincrop potatoes. French and runner beans can now go straight into the ground, as can sweetcorn. Start sowing beetroot, broccoli, chard, chicory and rocket outdoors, and continue sowing carrots, peas and salad crops.

PLANTING OUT Seeds sown in the greenhouse in early spring will be ready to transplant into your plot at the end of spring. If possible harden them off in a cold frame first, or protect them in a polytunnel once they're in the ground. New seedlings are vulnerable to pests, heavy rain, a late frost and harsh winds, so give them all the help you can. Setting slug traps is wise, as is surrounding each seedling with protective grit. The high winds at Cornworthy mean many plot holders use collars to protect their seedlings.

EARTHING UP POTATOES As your potatoes grow, they need earthing up. Simply draw up the soil around the plants to form a bank. This encourages the creation of more potatoes and protects the crop from airborne diseases such as blight.

PROTECTING STRAWBERRIES As the fruits start to ripen, put straw underneath your strawberries. This prevents the fruits coming into contact with the ground and rotting, and is a barrier for slugs. Cover with nets to protect from birds.

CLEARING UP Lift the last of your winter crops and either eat them or put on the compost heap. Brassica stumps take a long time to compost so chop them up before you add them to your heap.

Clockwise from left *Chive flowers taste as good as they look; use straw to keep strawberries out of reach of slugs; frilly lollo rosso lettuce adds a splash of colour; a globe artichoke, ready to harvest*

Pests and problems

Other gardeners and growers have many reasons to be jealous of the plot holders at Cornworthy: a long growing season, an inspiring view, a wonderful sense of community. But the single thing that will make more than fingers turn green is the fact that the Cornworthy plot doesn't have a slug problem. At least not yet…

'They haven't found us yet,' says Steve, the site manager, 'but they'll get here eventually. People will bring compost in from elsewhere and the few that are here will find plenty to feed on and start to breed. When that happens it will be like everywhere else, but these first two years we've been lucky.' Artichokes are unmolested. Lettuces are hole-free. Seedlings aren't consumed the day they poke their leaves through the soil. Slug-free growing: the holy grail of British gardening.

The lack of slugs has, however, contributed to the site's biggest problem: weeds, specifically docks. As the field was untended for years before the allotments were started, the docks went unchecked by machines as well as gastropods, and they have been very stubborn about going. The only solution, according to Steve, is to keep on weeding. He's often heard repeating the old saying 'One year's seeds, seven years' weeds', and tells growers that with constant hoeing, the plants will eventually weaken and become less of a problem. That assumes that everyone keeps their plot tidy, which, of course, not everyone does and can be a sore subject with those who do keep their weeds down.

It's been notable how the pests and problems are changing at Cornworthy as the plot becomes more established. In the first year, the fruit crops were left alone by the local birds, primarily because they hadn't discovered the booty on offer (and it helped that there was a sparrowhawk around). But in the second year, the birds learnt that the allotments produce a ready supply of food, and those plot holders who didn't net their fruit suffered losses. For the plot holders, there's a balance to be found between the effort required to net the fruit or accepting a certain amount of loss.

Paul Henderson, who's won 'best plot' two years in a row from the local gardening club, found the birds were also after his brassicas. 'Steve Hunt warned me he'd seen some pigeons swooping down on his plot like the RAF in formation to eat his brassica seedlings, so in and around my seedlings I stuck a whole load of sticks into the ground, and that stopped the pigeons from landing. It really wasn't very much work at all and I'll definitely do it again next year.'

The birds aren't the only pests that have learnt there's now more food in the field: there are mice and rabbits around who are only too happy to steal the plot holders' hard work from out of the ground. Although plenty of space has been left for the rabbits next to the hedges and every plot has been fenced off, a few of them have still found their way into the plots. The main weakness has been the gates, which obviously can't be sunk below the surface! The solution that seems to work is to bury a couple of bricks or breezeblocks under the threshold to stop them digging underneath.

The chain-link fences can't stop the mice though, and when food is scarce elsewhere, they start to investigate what the allotments have to offer. Broad beans that are planted late in autumn or early

A series of plastic hoops, positioned over rows of carrots, acts as a framework for fine netting to deter carrot root fly

in spring when there's little else in the ground seem to be a particular favourite for the mice, and as soon as they see a green shoot, they start digging for the bean itself. The solution is harsh: mousetraps.

Some of the brassica crops have been attacked by the caterpillars of the cabbage white butterfly, though the brassicas on the allotment have suffered far less than the ones the plot holders had previously grown at home. But as the years go on, the butterflies will find their way to the allotment field with increasing regularity. The second year saw the first appearance of sawfly at the plots: they only attacked the gooseberry bushes and thankfully only stripped them of their leaves after the fruits had been harvested.

As it's the Allotment Association's intention that the site is cultivated as organically as possible, no one wants to use insecticides or pesticides. A few plot holders use a mild soap spray, but there's another solution that is even more organic than that: simply pick off the caterpillars that are doing the damage. The squeamish don't have to worry about squishing them: by simply shaking the plant or picking the bugs off and leaving them on the ground you make it much easier for the birds to find them, and they'll do the squishing for you. That method works best, of course, if your patch is weed free so the birds can see the green insects against the brown earth.

Another of the Association's stipulations is that plot holders can't use hosepipes. Nearly 3,000 litres of water from the borehole are stored in tanks at the top of the site, and a gravity feed takes this down to smaller storage tanks around the field into which plot holders can dip their watering cans. Watering a 200-square metre plot with a watering can is a tedious and time-consuming job, but it's much easier for everyone than it was in the first year when there was just a single standpipe at one end of the field. The soil at Cornworthy is free draining and is prone to drying out. After a couple of warm weeks, it's easy to see who's done the hard graft with the watering can.

The big problem that almost everyone has had to deal with is the wind. It's an exposed site near the top of a hill, and if there isn't the prevailing south-westerly to deal with, there's a breeze coming in from the sea. All you can do is adapt your plot and your crops to compensate for the wind as much as possible. Most plots have some kind of windbreak, whether that's a cordon of fruit trees or a row of Jerusalem artichokes. Steve has planted an evergreen hedge of hardy – and inedible, of course – griselinia from cuttings and this will eventually protect his crops.

Tender plants are particularly vulnerable, with those planted out from their cosseted greenhouse existence being most at the mercy of the winds. Polytunnels keep out the wind, but they also stop the rain reaching the soil, which creates its own problems on a dry site. One answer has been to put plastic collars round individual plants until they're strong enough to survive on their own. Some people have also used their polytunnels as windbreaks between rows of seedlings rather than over them, thus protecting their crops and warming the ground for the next sowing.

The other way the good growers of Cornworthy have compensated for the wind is in their choice of crops. Tall climbing beans suffered so much in the first year that many people started experimenting with dwarf beans in the second year. Only reaching 45 centimetres in height, they're low enough and dense enough to withstand the odd blast and have cropped really well. Many more plot holders will be trying them in the years to come.

Clockwise from top left
Cabbage, netted for protection from birds; sweet peas supported on a frame of bamboo and netting; a plastic collar, made from a bottle, used to protect crops from pests and winds; peas are traditionally grown up twiggy sticks

Children

Children can spend many happy hours digging a little piece of earth, watering it and sometimes even planting something in it, and some of the Cornworthy families have set aside a small part of their allotment for their children to grow their own crops.

Find them a spot where they will have a chance of success: nothing is more likely to put them off than offering them the dark corner behind the shed where plants will never grow. And help them choose crops that they will enjoy seeing sprout up – as well as chow down – to engage their interest.

Plants that germinate and grow quickly are a good bet. Peas and beans are large enough to handle and soon emerge from the soil. And you can experiment with growing them in a glass at home (put a layer of damp kitchen paper round the inside of the glass and tuck the pre-soaked seeds between the paper and the glass).

Tomatoes are easy to grow, and striped varieties will add some drama. Children are often a little too enthusiastic about watering, which can lead to disappointment when their plants wilt and die as a result, but this is less likely to be a problem with tomatoes, courgettes and the pumpkin family, all of which need plenty of water while they are growing.

Courgettes, pumpkins and squash grow easily from seed, or you can buy plants if your children are impatient to see some progress. Squashes come in bright colours and interesting shapes, and pumpkins can be used for Hallowe'en celebrations. Everyone will be amazed at how big they grow, and it can be fun to enter the best of the produce at the local show.

Children love planting bulbs, even though they don't see anything happening for many months – but then the shoots are a great surprise when spring comes. Strawberries and soft fruit are universally popular, especially at harvest time, and sunflowers are always a success – and you can save the seeds for next year, or feed them to the birds.

Clockwise from top left *Cameron Simons at the Cornworthy garden show; Alex Harrigan enjoys a stroll through the allotments; Eloise Green checks flowers for earwigs; Cameron Simons and Eloise Green compare strawberry shapes*

Involve the children

" We live next door to Steve Hunt, so we knew we'd have to have an allotment, but I was daunted about taking on a whole plot. Steve persuaded me that looking after a full plot wasn't much more work than a half plot. Plus he said he'd give us a hand. He's helped my partner Matthew put the fencing up, and given us loads of plants and advice. We sectioned the plot broadly into three: at the bottom we've got the soft fruit; at the top we've got a lawned area with a picnic table and a mini-plot for the kids, Joe and Alex; and in the middle we've got all the veg. Even though it looks a mess we've still had loads of produce from it.

The onions have been very successful, as were the shallots and garlic. I've dried the garlic and probably have enough for the next six months. And the pumpkins have been great. There's something lovely about bringing your kids up to their own pumpkin patch in the days before Hallowe'en. I've tried to involve the kids as much as possible: they choose what to put on their bit of the plot, and the sunflowers have been great because they grow so quickly.

Don't think you've got to keep everything looking perfect, and don't try and keep up with those who do manage to keep their plots weed free. It doesn't matter if it's a mess if you go home with armfuls of veg.

The soft fruit has been a real success and we've grown white currants, blackcurrants, loganberries, tayberries, blueberries, rhubarb and gooseberries. We also put in a plum tree and a pear tree. We had punnets and punnets of strawberries from eight plants. We had so many I had to make jam. Last year it was courgettes. I made courgette cake, courgette and ginger jam, courgette chutney . . . I didn't realise I'd have to do so much cooking on top of all the gardening.

Matthew thinks a meal isn't complete without a potato, so we planted loads. I'd say we were self-sufficient. We rotated the crops round and left last year's potato patch fallow this year, but several plants have sprung up. If you don't get all the tubers out of the ground, they'll keep coming, so that's a bit of a bonus. It's been the same with the Jerusalem artichokes; I actually wish I hadn't put them in because they're everywhere and there's only so many you can eat.

The real problem we've had has been with the brassicas. There's a bit of clubroot in the field and the leaves have been feasted on by butterflies. I don't know if I'll grow them again, I'll see how everyone else gets on next year and then make a decision. The only other thing I'd do differently is plant some flowers. When you let your plot gets as weedy as this one, having something pretty to look at would make a difference. "

You can't do it all straight away

  ❝ I found the allotment a lot of work in the first year but it was the view that kept me going. After I'd got the fencing done, the first job was planting some fruit trees and building a couple of raised beds, but with my job and Elise to look after, finding the time for the allotment wasn't easy. I struggled: whenever I came back up here, the weeds had invaded the space I had cleared on my last visit. I was going to give up, because I thought it was unfair to other people, but then I had a word with Steve. He told me to take it slow and steady: you can't do it all straight away. It also helped that the people with plots either side also struggled. It's delinquents' row here, but knowing that I wasn't the only one who wasn't getting on top of things stopped me getting too down about it.

Steve suggested creating a grass area, which has been great for Elise. I usually bring a pop-up tent with me so she's got somewhere to play, and on a really hot day I even brought the paddling pool. There are often other kids up here and it's so safe that they go off and play together and I can get on with things. And of course, the grass area was one bit of the plot I had under control. Then Phil Green told me about weedproof fabric, which I have now covered one corner with. That's meant I've just had two beds to look after. Our garden at home is somewhere for Elise to play, and while she's young there won't be room to grow our own produce there, so this has been ideal. And getting to know people up here has been great. I knew perhaps three-quarters of the allotment holders before we started, but only by sight. I've got to know people really well up here, and there's usually someone to chat to, and there's always something to chat about!

It was the people and the view that convinced me to keep plugging away, and then around September time I was up here doing a bit of harvesting and something just clicked. The soil was warm between my fingers and it just smelt so good! It was invigorating and I thought that I'm just going to go for it. This autumn, I'm going to get another two raised beds built and double what I can grow here.

I gave a lot of thought as to what to grow, and decided not to bother with things that are cheap to buy. So I haven't planted onions or potatoes or carrots, because they're always in the shops and never expensive, and I often take a box from our local organic food supplier which has those staples in. Instead I've planted kale – which has been delicious – and beetroot, sweetcorn, tomatoes, squash, beans, Savoy cabbages and plenty of soft fruit.

The other day I came up here with Elise and she was really disappointed that there were no more strawberries. In this day and age when you can buy them all year round in the supermarket, I like the idea that she's learning about how things grow. Hopefully she's picking things up by osmosis and will be brilliant at this when she's older. ❞

Don't do the whole plot straight away, especially if you're new to growing. If it's too daunting to look after the whole lot, cover some of it in weedproof fabric or create a lawn until you've got a plot that feels manageable. Eventually you'll fill it up.

We're learning all the time

66 Our neighbour is a guy called Paul Hunt who – although he doesn't have a plot up here – was instrumental in getting this project off the ground and is the Association's treasurer. He asked us very early on if we wanted a plot and we said yes straight away.

There's no doubt it's a big time commitment, especially in the first year. We spent the first couple of months pulling stones out the ground and reading books about what to plant and when. But even in just our second year it's got easier: we know what we're doing a bit now and we don't have to look so much up in books – and the groundwork we did at the beginning is paying off.

We both work full time, so mostly it's been coming up at the weekends, but if one of us finishes work early, we'll come up here and get the hoe out, or give everything a good soak and pick whatever needs harvesting. It's probably three hours at the weekend, and half an hour or so a few evenings a week. It is a wonderful way to unwind after a day at work, and those evening sessions mean we keep on top of the weeds and nothing dries out.

At the weekends we're usually up here with our daughter Eloise, who's seven, and she's got her own corner of the plot. We asked her what she wanted to grow – last year it was vegetables, this year there are a lot of flowers – and we help her with it, but she definitely knows it's her patch. Especially because the strawberries are in her corner! Last year it was a fortnight before we got one because they never made it home. She would just sit here and eat them.

She likes picking tomatoes and mangetout and will even eat carrots straight from the ground. Her attention span isn't great – some of the time she'll get bored and want to go home – but she'll help out with weeding and watering and quite enjoys a spot of deadheading. She's also discovered that you can use marigolds to draw with, so her friends sometimes get marigold tattoos. Our son Josh, who's nineteen, mostly helps out with the eating side of things (although he was left in charge of the plot when we went on holiday). We had so many mangetout last year that they became his favourite TV snack.

We've discovered that some gluts are easier to deal with than others. You can't freeze lettuce, for instance, and there's only so much cauliflower you can eat before you start to hate it, so we've modified our planting in the second year and made a bigger effort with successional sowing. We actually got a second freezer last year because we were bringing so much home from the plot. Every other day there'd be another trugful of beans to trim and wash and

get in the freezer. We also had a lot of courgettes and we had to find new recipes to cope, but that was quite a fun challenge. We ate plenty of soup!

As well as the successional sowing, which has made a big difference this year, we learnt a few other things last year that we've put into practice. Like the netting on our brassicas: last year we had the cheap green stuff and it was a real pain to use. You'd pull on one end and the other would come loose, or it'd roll up into a ball and tear. We built proper supports for some heavy-duty netting this year and it's much easier to take on and off so we can get in there with a hoe; it's actually big enough for us to get on hands and knees and crawl underneath to do the weeding.

It's always interesting to see what other people are growing. In the first year, we were the only people to try growing tomatoes up here, and they were such a success – we had a lot of tomato soups and spaghetti sauces – that lots of people are trying them this year and we've done the same in reverse. That's the great thing about being up here, there's loads of inspiration – we're often swapping plants with other plot holders – and of course with Steve around there's always plenty of advice too. **"**

Little and often. Even if you can only pop up for half an hour, you can run a hoe between a couple of rows of veg and it will help keep everything under control. If nothing else needs doing, your crops will thank you for a water. If you do the weeding and watering in little stints, they don't seem like too much of a chore.

As the sun climbs
higher in the sky and
the hours of daylight
lengthen, plants
respond by putting
on a spurt of growth.
Summer is a time of
miraculous abundance,
when the only problem is
keeping up with the harvest

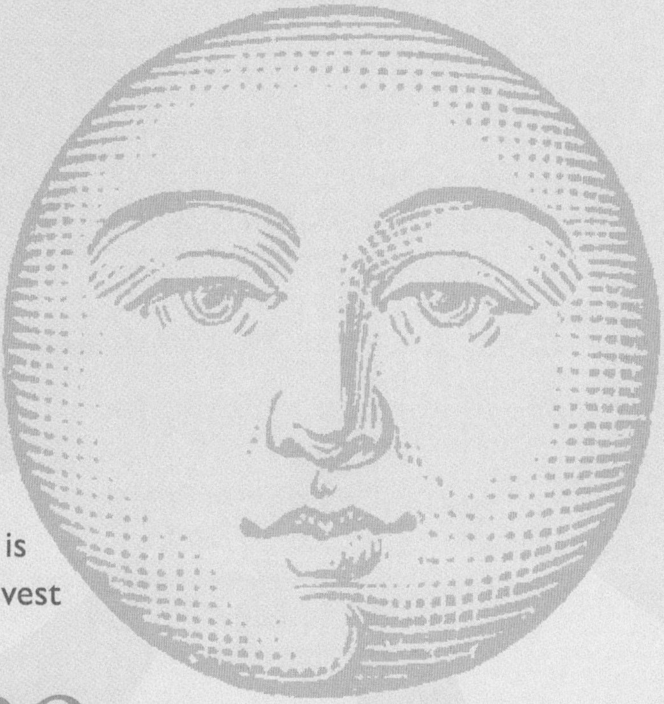

In the
summertime

What to do in summer

When the weather's warm, spending time in your allotment is a pleasure, especially as there's no heavy digging to do. The priority is to keep crops fed and watered while you continue with successional sowing. And you will need to make regular visits to keep on top of your harvesting.

Early summer

HARVESTING Broad beans that were planted before Christmas should start to offer up their first harvests near the end of June, as will established strawberries, if it's been a warm spring, and the first of the asparagus. Beans, peas and mangetout, spring cabbage, first early potatoes, lettuces, rocket, radishes and rhubarb should all be producing generously in early summer.

SOWING Seeds for cucurbits – pumpkins, squashes, cucumbers, marrows and courgettes – can go straight in the ground now. Continue sowing French and runner beans, beetroot, broccoli, carrots, peas, spinach, swedes, turnips and salad crops.

PLANTING OUT Bring out the remaining seedlings from the greenhouse. They will need less protection than those transplanted in the spring, but they will need plenty of water to help get them established. Leeks are best puddled in: make a hole with a dibber and place the baby leek in the hole, then simply pour water into the hole and let the resulting mud set the leek in place.

Young sweetcorn settling in for the summer

Left, top and bottom *Steve using a dibber to make holes for his leek seedlings, before puddling them in*

Below *A fine display of lupins with the River Dart in the distance*

Right *Peter Fowler and Helen Isitt, hoeing and watering their newly acquired plot*

PROTECTING SOFT FRUIT As fruit ripens, it needs to be netted to keep birds from helping themselves to your harvest. Keep an eye out for insects: shake sawfly larvae from fruit bushes so the birds can see them easily and use soapy water to keep greenfly and blackfly under control. As they ripen, raspberries and tomatoes may need additional canes to keep them from collapsing.

WEEDING It's not just your crops that thrive in summer – the weeds like the conditions too. Spend the first half hour at your plot with a hoe in your hand and you'll easily keep on top of them.

WATERING At this time of year gardeners pay special attention to the weather report. During dry spells, make extra trips to your allotment to ensure growing plants are getting enough moisture (tomatoes and the cucurbits, in particular, always need plenty of water).

Don't rely on the rain to give plants enough water. Rainfall in winter and rainfall in summer bring different benefits: a winter downpour is more likely to help the crops in the long term than one in summer, when plants lose as much water to the air as the heavens release. Mulching crops with manure or compost will help keep moisture in the soil, and reduce the need for watering.

PRUNING Stone fruit, such as apricots, peaches and plums, are pruned at this time of year, rather than in late autumn or late winter. (However, young stone fruit trees are best pruned in early spring, just as the buds burst.)

Left *Salad crops are plentiful at this time of year*

Opposite, clockwise from top left *Peas; sweet peas; new potatoes; rhubarb and broad beans; raspberry*

Late summer

HARVESTING Late summer is an abundant time. Aubergines, beans, beetroot, brassicas, carrots, courgettes, cucumbers, marrows and some squashes, peppers, spinach, sweetcorn, salad crops and tomatoes will be ready. Lift onions and leave to dry on the soil for a couple of weeks before storing in a cool shed. Second early potatoes will be ready, as will raspberries, blackberries and some varieties of apple.

SOWING OUTDOORS July is your last chance to sow winter root crops such as parsnips and carrots. Sow runner and French beans for a late crop in the autumn, possibly on the site of the first early potatoes, which will be lifted by now. When your early beans are finished, winter brassicas will benefit from the nitrogen the legumes will have left in the soil.

FEEDING Mulch fruit bushes and beans with manure or compost. Make a comfrey feed by leaving a big net of comfrey leaves and stinging nettles in a water butt for a couple of weeks and use the liquid undiluted.

WATERING Don't forget to water, even if it rains. Established plants respire gallons of water a day when it's warm, so crops are always thirsty in summer.

GOING ON HOLIDAY If you are going away for a couple of weeks, ask another plot holder if they can keep your plot watered and check for pest infestations. Before you go, harvest as much as you can and freeze and preserve where possible. Pull yellowing leaves off brassicas and salads to discourage slugs. Let other plot holders know if you're happy for them to harvest while you're away, or harvest crops that are likely to ripen while you are away and put them on the compost heap, as rotten crops left in situ will encourage pests. Don't forget to water thoroughly before you go.

Clockwise from top left
Red cherries; basket of colourful produce; fresh lettuce

LOOKING AFTER STRAWBERRIES Once strawberries have stopped fruiting they send out runners. Cut these off, along with some of the outer leaves, so that the plant's energy goes into making it stronger. Give plants a good mulch to aid this process. Strawberry plants are good for four or five seasons: after that, let the runners put roots down and make new plants, and then lift and compost the original plant.

Left *Steve Hunt picking his strawberries*

Opposite, clockwise from left
Freshly picked strawberries taste wonderful; mature strawberry plants, with the protective netting removed; strawberries and cream at the Cornworthy pig roast

Fork to fork

The Cornworthy plot holders spend, on average, between three and six hours a week on their allotments. In addition to those hours, there are several more spent in the kitchen, because once you've grown your own, you've got to cook your own too. There really isn't any doubt that having an allotment changes the way you eat.

Many allotmenteers talk of the sheer joy of sitting down to a meal made up entirely of things they've grown themselves. Preparing and cooking crisp, fresh veg bursting with flavour is rarely a chore, but once you've had eight weeks of courgettes, or broad beans, or sweetcorn or beetroot, the novelty of eating in tune with the seasons starts to lose some of its appeal. Gone are the days of picking up what you fancy from the supermarket: you now have to eat whatever your plot has given you.

Successional sowing can keep unwanted gluts to a minimum, but as the weather improves throughout the spring, crops grow more quickly and plants sown weeks apart eventually start to mature at the same time. When you have grown the glut yourself, when you understand the effort and time (and no small amount of heartache) required to produce a harvest, chucking out your excess is not an option. You just can't bring yourself to do it, and so you have to find a new way of cooking your crop. If you want to grow your own, you've got to get canny in the kitchen.

New allotment holders are often bought books by friends and family on growing veg, but what they really need are recipe books. Although it's time-consuming, most of the Cornworthy growers have found the kitchen challenges have brought out their creative side: courgettes are no longer typecast as a component of ratatouille, suddenly they've been given a starring role in everything from cakes to chutneys, even becoming a meal in themselves, cored out, stuffed and roasted until they are meltingly soft.

When people take an allotment, they often hope they are saying goodbye to the weekly shop, but they soon realise that, once they've found a recipe

Below Young marrows, partly hidden in the shadows, start to gain weight

Opposite, clockwise from top Courgette flowers ripe for eating; rounded rosette of cabbage leaves; mangetout ready for harvest

to use up their spaghetti squash or purple sprouting broccoli, they still need to buy the rest of the ingredients to make a meal. The asparagus spears they've harvested might be heavenly with a knob of butter and a twist of black pepper, but perhaps they could be equally good with some salmon, or chicken or bacon as well.

The truth is that once you are growing fruit and vegetables, you really start to care about them, and that means part of your brain never quite switches off from thinking about them. It's not only the weather forecast that growers start watching out for, it's also the recipe sections in newspapers and magazines. What if I substituted that ingredient with beetroot? I wonder if that sauce would work well with my cauliflowers? An allotment doesn't just take up your time: it can also take over your imagination.

If there's one cooking skill that every gardener with even the tiniest of vegetable plots needs to master it is, of course, the ability to make a good soup. Not only will soup use up almost anything you've got, it will also wait quite happily in the freezer until you can bear to let another leek/beetroot/pumpkin pass your lips!

Above *Ripe blackcurrants*

Right *Beetroot for sale at the Cornworthy pig roast*

Opposite *Sweetcorn loses its flavour fast once picked – you can't get better than home-grown*

The flowers put on a colourful display throughout the summer months

Flowers

An allotment is the ideal place to grow flowers for cutting. Harvesting them will not affect the display in your flower beds and you can experiment with colours that might not fit in with your garden planting scheme.

Flowers that are suitable for taking home are ideally long stemmed and long lasting when cut. Sweet peas are often grown on a framework of canes, producing quantities of delicate, sweet-smelling pastel blooms which flower more profusely the more they are picked. Dahlias are robust and brightly coloured, flowering later in the year – just in time for the autumn show.

Bulbs are good candidates for allotment planting: their dying leaves can look unsightly in the garden, but on the plot they can be left undisturbed and will increase in number over the years. As well as traditional daffodils and narcissi in yellow and white, there are tulips in a huge array of colours, graceful lilies and gaudy gladioli, and garlic-scented alliums with their curious globes.

There are also many brightly coloured annuals and more subdued perennials that will give lasting pleasure both on the allotment and in the home. But flowers aren't just for sticking in vases: they attract bees and other pollinators to your plot, some can lure predators away from your crops, and a few are even edible. Sunflowers are popular with everyone, including birds and bees, and nasturtiums and marigolds are easy to grow, bright and cheerful, and can be eaten in salads (assuming you haven't used pesticides near them).

And don't forget that vegetables can be decorative too: asparagus fronds are prized by flower arrangers, and onions and chives produce pretty flowers when they are allowed to go to seed.

Left *Use flowers to attract essential pollinators, such as bees, to your plot. Sweet peas and dahlias are good lures and look stunning too*

Opposite, clockwise from top left *Sweet Williams; tulips; lilies; sunflowers*

PLOT HOLDER'S TALES: Sheryle Boughton

Don't be afraid to grow flowers

" My husband Michael thought we could be virtually self-sufficient if we took over a whole plot, and he did really well with the edible crops in our first year, but I still wanted to grow flowers so I asked Elizabeth to let me know if anyone gave up a half plot. It was suggested that – because our plot is at the edge of the field – we could add a half plot to our existing plot. So in the second year, that's exactly what we did.

I divided the flower plot into three and in one third I have a wild flower garden, in another third I have really traditional cottage garden plants like hollyhocks and foxgloves, and the final third a few fruit trees and spring bulbs. It's the wild flower area that people seem to like, and it's very special to me. Whenever I've moved house, I have collected seeds from the flowers in my old garden and taken them with me to the new one. As our own garden wasn't ready for planting, I simply took my plastic bag of old seeds up to the allotment and scattered them. I didn't do anything else apart from watering them and they have produced so many flowers. From May to September they've been beautiful to look at, both up at the allotment and in vases around our house.

When Christine Walkden came to visit, I really didn't want to show her my plot because it wasn't looking its best. But someone said Christine had seen it and wanted to talk to me, and I thought, I can't have a TV gardener looking at my plot and not ask for some advice! So I asked her what I should do to my mini-meadow to get the most out of it next year. Her advice was to do absolutely nothing, not even strim it down in the spring. She says it will all seed by itself, and apart from pulling out the odd vigorous weed like the thistles, I should let nature take its course. I do worry that letting it self-seed might be good for me but might mean more weeds for our neighbours. We're lucky that the people with surrounding plots are very diligent weeders, but I have said to Elizabeth that if it is an issue for anyone then I'll stop. Certainly the only comments I get from other plot holders are positive. We don't enter the allotment or produce competitions, but someone told me that if we did then she'd vote for our plot: I was really quite touched by that.

The flowers look beautiful but they also attract beneficial wildlife. Steve told me that he saw something in my plot the other day and went to investigate and it was a pheasant chick, and I thought, at least if it's eating my seeds it's leaving everyone else's crops alone. "

A friend back where we used to live has an allotment and she says that there's no community spirit on her site. The social side of things makes such a difference, so if you don't know the person at the next plot, I'd say go up and introduce yourself, because it's a great way to get to know people.

Leave space to hoe

66 Although I knew most of the people who have a plot, I've got to know them even better since I started seeing them up here every week. My plot is right in front of the shed, so it tends to be very sociable. In the village you get the people who go to the pub, the people who go to the church and organisations like the WI and they tend not to mix, but up here you get to meet everyone. Kids with young families, people from some of the neighbouring villages, people I wouldn't meet otherwise.

I knew I wanted to grow flowers up here because I love having them in the house and obviously I don't want to pick the ones in my garden. I have half a plot, and I thought I wouldn't have much room for vegetables, but as there are only the two of us at home we don't need tons of stuff. This is the right amount of space for us. At the start it was really hard work: there were barrowfuls of manure and material to be brought in, and I was very glad I was right next to where we park the cars. Once all the preparation had been done, I was pretty haphazard about where I planted things. I know some people make plans, and keep a list and then rotate them. I'm just relying on memory to know where to move things to next year.

I hadn't anticipated the excitement of growing your own. When seeds start to germinate you can't quite believe it, and when I came up here and saw my first baby courgette I was just so thrilled. It amazes me that something so big can come from such a tiny seed.

I learnt a lot in my first year and the harvest has been a bit better in the second year. For instance, I knew the winds up here could do damage, so this year I've put in dwarf beans and they've been brilliant. The gooseberries have been much better this year too, and I know now that's because fruit bushes don't produce much of a crop in their first year. I planted my onions too close together and they're impossible to weed; next year I'll make sure they're a hoe's width apart.

Without a doubt the hardest thing has been the weeding. They say it will get better as the years go on and the weeds get weakened by our efforts, and I can't wait. Once you've spent two hours weeding, you don't have much time or energy left for planting. But the entire site is now producing so much veg that we're talking about how we can distribute it. By law you can't sell produce from allotments, but we're thinking about leaving our gluts somewhere in the village with an honesty box to raise funds for the Association or the village hall. There are lots of people in the village who would like to grow their own but who are too busy or maybe a bit frail, so if we can share our gluts with them that would be great. I'd love to share my excess with my neighbour, but as Jenny (*on right in main photo*) has the other half of my plot, she's usually got a glut of her own to deal with. 99

You don't have to have any special knowledge to grow crops. It's pretty much just common sense. You can follow the rules you read in books or you can just put some seeds in the ground and see what happens!

Other people's plots are really educational

❝ I've only got a half plot, which is fine because I'm very busy with work, and I study with the OU and sing in the choir, and this is probably all I could manage. I work just across the road, so I come here in my lunch hour. Very often there's no one else around, so I have a good look at what everyone else is doing. I've gardened at home, but there's so much I don't know about growing fruit and veg and it's really educational to see what other people are doing. It's reassuring that people are having the same battles with weeds and the wind, but it's also inspiring to see what they are managing to produce. I always take a look at Steve's plot because that way I know what to do next. If I see him feeding, or pruning, or whatever, then I copy as best I can.

I inherited my plot from someone who moved away, and all sorts of wonderful things keep popping up – pretty flowers and lots of fruit – which is lucky for me because you tend to get better harvests after the first year. The fencing had already been done, but my husband Patrick came up and laid paths for me, so I've now got four planting areas which means I'll be able to rotate my crops.

My favourite vegetable is purple sprouting broccoli and my second is leeks. A friend recommended perpetual spinach and I was harvesting within about two weeks of planting, and it's been non-stop ever since. The broad beans were also easy to grow, though the most successful ones were the plants I started off in the lean-to at home. I think the wind was just too much for the seedlings up here. I was convinced the sweetcorn wouldn't grow for the same reason. I bought a tray of baby plants from the market and they were stunted for a while, but they did well in the end. Unless something freezes easily I'd rather give it away. I don't have time for bottling or pickling or jam making. The great thing about going back to the office with my produce is that I can get rid of a glut. I was very popular with my colleagues during the strawberry season!

I get mesmerised when I come up here. I say I'll just do an hour, but suddenly it's three hours later. I haven't been organised enough to keep a diary, but I intend to take photos of the plot to remind myself what went where. And that will have the benefit of reminding me, when it's all back to bare earth in the winter, that all the hard work pays off. ❞

Be realistic about how much time you have, especially at the beginning. I'm sure I'll get better, and faster, but this first year it's taken three hours a week most weeks, and certainly a lot more than that at the beginning when we were doing the groundwork.

Community spirit

It's been ten years since Cornworthy lost its last shop. While there are plenty of activities to get involved with in the village – from amateur dramatics to a choir, the parish council and bell-ringing – the only places to meet your neighbours on a regular basis are the Hunters Lodge pub and the church. For those who take religion and alcohol in small doses, the allotments have provided a new focal point for meeting up and having a chat.

Villages with few public facilities and non-existent public transport can be quite isolating places, especially if you are at home all day caring for kids or elderly parents or working from the spare room. For a few plot holders at Cornworthy, the allotments have provided the motivation to get out of the house, and once they're up at the allotments, there's usually someone to talk to, and always something to talk about.

Even those villagers who knew most of the other plot holders before the project acknowledge that they have got to know their neighbours much better through the allotments. People they might previously have waved to across the street are now the people they stop and have a chat with. *How are your cabbages? Do you want my excess seed? I hear the weather's going to be bad this weekend. Are you entering anything in the garden show?*

The plot holders exchange gossip as well as leftover seedlings and techniques for planting out leeks or netting broccoli. A strawberry plant is swapped for a pumpkin. A few hours' help with the digging is rewarded with a share of the harvest or a pint in the pub. The spirit of generosity with which the project started when the landowner offered the field has continued as the seasons have come and gone.

The Cornworthy Allotment Association sees the allotments as something that benefits the entire community, not just the twenty-three plot holders. At the village fete, where everyone in Cornworthy takes part in games and a whole pig gets roasted on a spit, the Association had a produce stall and donated the takings to the village hall. It also auctioned a box of produce to the highest bidder,

Opposite *Elizabeth Sherwood (left) and Sophie Tucker would be the first to agree that alongside the plants, friendship and community spirit grow on the Cornworthy allotments*

and the winner had a box of allotment produce delivered to their door once a week throughout the summer.

In the summer of 2011, the Association threw a party to celebrate the drilling of the borehole, as this marked the completion of the original plan to be self-sufficient. All the grant givers, plot holders, families and friends were invited to the shed for drinks and samples of the field's wares. Despite some pretty rubbish weather, plenty of people were still making merry in the wee small hours before stumbling down the hill to the village.

Of course, Cornworthy was a pretty special kind of a place to start with. There could be all sorts of reasons for this: the lack of second homes is seen as significant, as is the fact that it is still a working village with a mix of ages and classes. Artists, writers, farm workers, retired diplomats, health workers, civil servants, teachers . . . it's as diverse as it's friendly. Unlike some rural communities that have a slightly feudal air – with a big house for the gentry, a slightly smaller one for the clergy and a few rows of cottages for the workers – Cornworthy is a much more egalitarian sort of village. New residents are made to feel welcome and residents are invited – but never pressured – to get involved in the village's organisations and activities. It's not a surprise that a village like Cornworthy has successfully arranged its own allotment association, but it has been surprising to discover just how much closer together the allotments have brought the residents of the village.

Clockwise from top left
The Cornworthy allotments barbecue, held at the allotment site; Steve Shepherd manning the barbecue; Sue and Michael Stevenson, stalwarts of Cornworthy; Tom Hartnell, Cornworthy farmer; Peter Fowler, Alun Sherwood, Steve Hunt and Michael Boughton enjoying the day

The Cornworthy pig roast, held in the Priory field in the middle of Cornworthy. **Clockwise from above** David Carver, Rupert Keane and Richard Porritt carving the pig; view from Priory field of the village; tug of war gets under way with an unknown canine helper; Paul Hunt weighs his beetroot; competitors for the dog show are eager to join in

At the turning point of the year, there is
a glorious blaze of colour and a plentiful
harvest of fruit for the autumn larder
before the season begins to move,
exhausted, towards the quiet of winter

Autumn leaves, berries and fruit

What to do in autumn

Autumn is a busy time in the allotment: there's still plenty to harvest and, as soon as crops give up the ghost, there's a big clear-up operation to get done before winter sets in. If you've had a glut of squashes, potatoes or root crops, you'll also need to find time to prepare these crops for storing. Dealing with an apple glut is a common problem at this time of year, but if you can press your apples, the juice can be frozen and stored – or you could do what they do in Devon and have a go at making cider. If, that is, you have the time…

Clockwise from left
Pumpkins ready for Hallowe'en; a small present of runner beans; well-scrubbed carrots; dramatically coloured chard

AUTUMN LEAVES, BERRIES AND FRUIT

HARVESTING The apples and pears that have looked tempting for the past few months will finally be ripe enough to pick, though most varieties taste better after they've been stored for a couple of weeks. At ground level, pumpkins of all shapes, colours and sizes will be ready for picking, and the brassicas, spinach, carrots and other root crops should be cropping heavily now. Maincrop potatoes should still be delivering harvests.

PLANTING You can still plant some crops now for a harvest this year, such as winter varieties of spinach and some hardy lettuces (though they will need the protection of a polytunnel when winter comes).

FEEDING If your runner beans are still going, give them a liquid feed to get a late harvest out of them.

CLEARING UP As plants stop producing, cut them down and throw them on the compost heap so that you can dig over the ground. Tidy up the greenhouse and disinfect surfaces, tools and pots thoroughly.

SOWING GREEN MANURES As you clear each patch of your allotment, broadcast seed for one of the many green manures available. These are crops such as ryegrass, mustard and fodder radish which are rich in nutrients and are sown on fallow ground, to improve the soil's fertility and workability. Sowing green manures will cover the ground and prevent weeds taking over. It will also insulate the soil from the worst of the cold. In early spring, simply dig the plants into the soil, where they will add valuable fibre and nutrients.

Clockwise from far left
Juicy plums – pick them before the birds get them!; rosy red apples in abundance; raspberries hiding under the leaves; autumn bounty – apples collected in a wicker basket; green tomatoes

Late autumn

HARVESTING Late varieties of potatoes will be offering up their last crop and any tubers stored in the ground should be lifted and stored in a cool, dark shed or cupboard. Tender leeks will need eating before the frosts come. Beans, brassicas, cucurbits, hardy salad crops and perpetual spinach will still be producing.

STORING Lift all your remaining pumpkins and root crops and store them. Carrots can be stored in the ground until the frosts come (lift them, then bury them in a corner of your plot). Squashes will keep for months in a shed or cool cupboard.

PLANTING Put in broad beans, garlic and spring cabbages now for an early crop next year, though you will need to protect them from animals as other food sources dwindle. Place fleece or polytunnels over your winter crops to protect them if there's an early cold snap forecast.

IMPROVING THE SOIL If you have a heavy soil, the most important thing to do at this time of year is to turn over your plot before the ground freezes, digging in plenty of well-rotted manure or home-made compost. Or you can leave a thick layer (5–8 centimetres) of manure on top of the soil as a mulch, and let nature (and the worms) do the work. Light soils are best dug in late winter or spring.

Digging at this time of year means that the soil is exposed to the cold weather: frost might be bad for most crops, but it is great for soil and acts as a cleansing agent. Frost also breaks down clods of earth into a tilth, making digging in early spring much easier.

LIMING If your brassicas have been affected by clubroot, or a soil test reveals your soil has become acidic, scatter handfuls of lime into the soil and dig in, following the instructions on the packet. (If you forget to do this in the autumn, or don't have the time, you can lime in winter instead.) Leave the lime to work for at least a month before adding organic

matter to this part of your plot. Even if you haven't had clubroot, liming the patch where you plan to grow brassicas next year will improve the quality and quantity of your cauliflowers, cabbages, broccoli and sprouts.

PRUNING AND PROPAGATING When the leaves start to fall in late autumn, it's time to prune apple and pear trees, to maintain shape and vigour. Take cuttings of hardwood fruit bushes like gooseberries and currants and propagate under glass. Cut raspberry canes down to just above ground level.

CLEARING UP As plants start to wilt and die, pick off dead and dying leaves, as this will take away hiding places and food for slugs. Clean and store plant supports for next year. Cut down asparagus, artichokes and any other permanent plants, and put the pruned foliage on the compost heap.

Storing

It's a wonderful feeling to walk through your front door with a trugful of fresh, healthy and tasty produce that you've grown yourself. All the aches and pains of bending and digging melt away when you gaze down at your verdant hoard. And then it hits you: you're sick of courgettes and the freezer is already full of beans and raspberries. It's not long after your first harvest that new gardeners realise the importance of good storage.

Several plot holders at Cornworthy have acquired second freezers to handle the amount of produce they harvest, while others have discovered talents for chutney and jam making, or researched recipes for sauces and soups to help them make the most of their hard work. Here are some of the ways they have kept enjoying their harvest long after they brought their bounty home.

- **SOFT FRUIT** This freezes well, and all you have to do is wash it and put it in a bag. It can also be turned into jams, pie fillings and sauces that can be stored for several weeks in airtight jars.

- **TREE FRUIT** Most varieties of apple and pear taste better once they have been stored for a couple of weeks, but this is not always the case, so you may need to experiment for the first few years. The key to good storage is a cool, even temperature (so a shed that is still getting hot in the autumn is not a good idea) and ventilation to prevent rotting. If you store your fruit in specially designed racks, your autumn harvest should still be edible in late spring.

- **POTATOES** The best place to store potatoes is often in the ground. Once the foliage starts to yellow, cut it down to the ground and leave the tubers in the soil until you're ready to eat them. However, if the soil is waterlogged, unusually warm, or prone to the tiny keel slugs that feed on potatoes, you'll need to lift and store the crop. Simply knock off the worst of the soil, put the potatoes in hessian sacks and leave in a cool, dark place (a garage or dry cellar is ideal). Lift all potatoes before the frosts come and store them indoors.

- **ROOT CROPS** Many of these can be stored in the soil. To prevent them continuing to grow and getting tough, lift them, cut off their leaves and bury them in an unused corner of your plot – assuming, of course, that you don't have a slug problem, in which case you are just leaving out a meal for your worst enemy! Most crops need to be lifted before the frosts, though parsnips are quite happy in the ground all winter (but it can be difficult to dig them out if the ground is frozen). Once lifted, store in racks in a cool, dark place.

Ripe apples in the evening sun

LEGUMES Peas and beans are best frozen as soon as they are picked. Shell, wash, top and tail as required and bag them up. There's some debate as to whether tougher beans are best parboiled (and allowed to cool) before freezing. It probably comes down to individual taste.

LEEKS Leeks are quite happy in the ground all winter, though they can be difficult to harvest when the ground is frozen. Some plot holders have found that, in winter, they can leave picked leeks in a shady spot outside their back door in a trug or box and they will be quite happy until the snows come.

ONIONS Leave onions to dry outside for a couple of weeks – simply lay them down on the spot where they were growing – before storing in nets and placing in a cool, dark place. Well-stored onions can last for up to nine months.

BRASSICAS Sprouts are happy to be left on your allotment throughout the winter until you're ready to eat them, as are cabbages. Broccoli can be prepared and frozen, while the best storage option for cauliflower is to cook it, put it in a pie and freeze the pie. If you're left with too many brassicas at the end of the growing season, try and give them to friends and neighbours, or they may just have to go on your compost heap.

PUMPKINS AND COURGETTES Courgettes need to be sliced and cooked if you want to freeze them successfully, though they are probably better used in chutneys and sauces and then frozen. When pumpkins have got to the desired size, simply cut them from the plant, leave them out in the sun for a couple of weeks (on a windowsill or in a greenhouse is ideal). Once they sound hard when you tap them, they are ready for storage. Packing them into crates lined with straw and then putting them in a cool, dark place seems to work well.

Best in show

Most people have an image of a village produce show in their head. Ruddy gardeners stand nervously next to plates of perfect, polished produce as judges peer over half-moon glasses, suck on their teeth and make tutting noises. And once the prized rosettes have been handed out, one can imagine it all getting a bit *Midsomer Murders* as tempers flare at the injustice of an overlooked turnip or surreptitiously swapped marrow. It is simultaneously a lot of fun, and a wee bit of stress.

Steve Hunt is the chairman of the local Cornworthy and Ashprington Garden Club, which has an annual awards event for its members and in 2010 created a new category: Best Allotment. Some plot holders knew there was no point in entering their patch, some were keen to give it a go, and some had their plots entered into the competition by their spouses without them knowing.

There is always a little bit of competitiveness between allotment holders, even without an organised competition. People walk past other plots and say to themselves, 'Oh, his beans are doing better than mine, but at least my sweetcorn is taller.' Some plot holders have realised they cannot possibly compete, but among those with the tidiest and productive plots, there are hints that they are trying to keep up with the Joneses.

The competition is judged by someone from a neighbouring garden club and for two years in a row, Paul Henderson has won the prize for the best plot. Paul's plot is definitely tidier and more productive than most of the others, which is no doubt because he puts in the hours. However, there is a suspicion that his modesty belies a steely determination to bag the first prize. 'He leaves his veg in there so it gets really big and impresses the judges,' says one of his fellow plot holders. 'His parsnips look good,' says another, 'but you'd need a chainsaw to get through them.' Clearly, vegetable competitions are a serious business.

In addition to the garden club awards, there is also the annual village show, where plot holders

The Cornworthy and Ashprington Garden Club competition, held in Cornworthy village hall

compete with other gardeners in the village for the best produce awards. The rules are pretty straightforward, but also pretty strict. For some crops – such as beans and potatoes – you have to offer the judges three specimens of similar size, shape and colour. For others, like the pumpkins, size is the important factor. And for those who know their produce is never going to win, there is always the Best Scarecrow award, which – usually – gets the children involved, although much of the work seems to get done long after they have gone to bed.

Julie Green decided she'd take the plunge and enter some of her vegetables for scrutiny and consideration. 'The night before I sat at home trying to find three potatoes that were roughly the same size and roughly the same shape, and I did the same with the runner beans and the onions. I was quite pleased with what I put in.' On the day of the competition, however, she realised just how seriously some people took it. 'I knew you were supposed to dress your veg up, pulling off the outer skin of your onions, but I didn't realise that there were tricks you could use. Everyone else had these perfectly straight runner beans, and it was only afterwards that I learned they'd all wrapped theirs in a damp tea towel overnight which – I now know – helps you straighten them. The towel also helps them keep their moisture in so they make just the right noise when the judges snap them. I had no idea.'

Even though it's just a bit of fun, there's no denying that the winners and runners-up are secretly quite chuffed. When you've raised a plant from seed to harvest, when you've taken care of it through frost and storms and drought, it's understandable that producing something that is both good to look at and good to eat makes you feel, well, a teeny bit proud.

Above *A visitor engrossed in the parish notes*

Left *Carrots, perfectly displayed*

Opposite, clockwise from top left *The exotic silverware for the winners; Sallie Johnston arranges her beans; has Vivienne Turner won 1st prize?; immaculate red onions are sure to impress the judges*

Begin with easy crops

“ It's a complete fluke that Anne Shepherd and I are next-door neighbours up here as well as in the village. I took over the other half of the plot when the original holder got posted overseas. Being next to Anne is fantastic, but she's such a good gardener – she's won awards from the gardening club for her garden at home – that I knew I couldn't compete. She has so many flowers on her plot and it looks so pretty. Whenever I come to my plot, I see Anne's first and I feel very uplifted.

One of the first things I did was put in some fruit trees. I've got an apple, a peach, a cherry and a plum. I've also put in a kiwi tree. The variety is called 'Jenny', so I had to give it a go. It's looking a little sorry for itself at the moment, but hopefully in a few years I might get some fruit on it.

The big successes have been the spinach, the sweetcorn and the mangetout. I had loads of broad beans, a good crop of potatoes and some lovely courgettes. I have a greenhouse at home, so I've started a few things off from seed, but I also bought some plug plants at the market in Totnes. I love coming up here before a meal and picking what I need. The other week I cooked for friends, and everything on the plate apart from the meat had come from here. It's a lovely feeling. I don't think you can overemphasise it. You can go into the shops and get a punnet of much smarter looking strawberries, but it's not the same as your own little strawberries. I remember the day I picked my first mangetout: I was over the moon. And harvesting potatoes? That was really quite magical. I got a whole bag from each seed potato and it was like finding buried treasure.

The only real problem I've had has been watering. It's been so dry that before we got the borehole I even brought up a dustbin of water in the back of the car, which was a bit of a risk, but it kept my crops alive.

It's very social up here. I often come in my van – I call it a van, but it's really a motorhome – and I can put the kettle on and stop and have a chat with someone. And there is always something to talk about and something to learn. The other week Elizabeth showed me how to puddle my leeks in, and she'd just learnt how to do it the week before from Steve.

I find that I lose myself up here. You just don't realise the time, and it's wonderful to be so absorbed in something that you don't think about anything else. It's very therapeutic in that way. I grew up in Africa and as a consequence I have a love of big open spaces and big scenery, which might explain why I feel so good up here. You can see the sea, the moor and it changes all the time as the sun moves over or a weather front comes in. In the summer, there's usually something cold and alcoholic in the fridge, and after a few hours' hard graft, sitting down with a friend and a drink to look at the view, well, it's good for the soul, isn't it? ”

Start off with some really easy crops to build your confidence.

Anyone can grow spinach. Broad beans are a doddle.

Potatoes take care of themselves.

It's so exciting that you'll

want to try more and

more each year.

Preparation pays dividends

❝ When I first moved here twenty-one years ago, there was a lot more farming in the village. I used to say that you'd see your next pint of milk being walked down the high street, but there's not so much of it now, so it's nice that in some way we're maintaining that link with the land. My dad used to grow his own. When he came out of the navy he got a job as a coastguard, and he dug up the front garden of the coastguard's cottage, then the back garden and then finally the neighbour's garden, and at one point he started selling veg to local hotels. It wasn't that unusual for men of his generation to grow enough to feed a family.

Last year I would say we were self-sufficient for about seven months of the year. Before I planted anything, I worked out two things: what we eat most of and how much we eat of those things. So, I estimated we ate around 250 to 300 onions a year, and I planted 300 onions. I lifted them in July and we were still eating them in March. I just stored them in crates in the garage. We quickly ran out of freezer space – we got a chest freezer in time for our second harvest – so we had to learn all sorts of preservation techniques that everyone would have known in the past. It's good fun finding recipes for your glut and you eat so much more healthily. In these days of growing obesity and diabetes, the more you visit your allotment, the less you'll see your doctor. There's the health benefits of being out in the fresh air, of getting the exercise – and it's not just physical health because it's good for your head, too.

In that first winter, I came up here a lot. I remember the snow clouds coming across from Dartmoor and big flakes falling, but I wanted to get it all dug over before the ground got too hard. I decided to double dig and add as much manure as I could. My wife kept saying, 'You're not going up there again are you?', but it does take a lot of time to prepare the site.

I divided the plot up into six beds – two for permanent crops and four for the rotational crops – and I reckon each bed took about fifteen hours to dig. But I pulled up enough stones to pave my paths, and I exposed a lot of weeds to the cold, which helped to suppress them when spring came. It was really hard, claggy work and my back was pretty shattered by the end of it. It was only when I stuck the fork in the ground and practically broke my wrist that I decided it was time to sit down with the seed catalogues. That was in January.

I do this primarily to provide food, but my wife thought I'd put in so much effort that she entered me in the competition for best plot. It was organised by the local gardening club, and a judge came over from Strete. I've always had this dread of veg competitions, but it was a bit of fun, and it was quite nice to win. I suppose, if I'm honest, I was a little bit proud. I really think the work I put in that first winter has already paid dividends. It got most of the stones out, it weakened the weeds and it broke the ground up for drainage and added all that organic matter and that's what's helped the crops to do so well. ❞

Cornworthy timeline

DECEMBER 2008
Letter written to parish council requesting the provision of allotments

MARCH 2009
Disappointment: the Association fails in its bid to use a local field

JULY 2009
Work begins on clearing the field of dead trees and its carpet of docks

SEPTEMBER 2009
The Association signs a ten-year lease agreement on Upper Slade field. Local farmers help with equipment and expertise and the field is ploughed and sectioned into seventeen plots measuring 20 × 10 metres

JANUARY 2009
Cornworthy Allotment Association established with a founding committee of six people, meeting in the Hunters Lodge pub in the village

JUNE 2009
A chance meeting between a committee member and a local landowner leads to a new offer of a field

OCTOBER 2009
Tenants move in, fence off their plots and prepare the ground

JANUARY 2010
Planning permission
obtained for the erection
of a communal shed and
composting toilet

AUTUMN 2010
Three further plots added,
due to demand. There is
now a waiting list for plots

SPRING 2010
Grants received from local councils and
organisations to pay for the shed, toilet,
straw-bale urinal and solar-powered borehole

SUMMER 2011
The borehole is drilled and solar-
powered pump is installed. The
allotments are now fully sustainable

Index

Note: Page numbers in **bold** indicate major sections, those in *italic* illustrations the subjects of which are not mentioned in accompanying text.

Afterword

" It is a magical experience to witness the journey a seed takes from planting, through germination, to fruition and finally to food on a plate.

When I heard that a field nearby was to be the home for the village allotments, it was an opportunity to photograph the stages of this journey and the transformation of an empty field into a productive project.

What I had not anticipated was the community spirit that the allotments would generate. There are no boundaries inside the allotment site – fences are for keeping out rabbits, not people. The plants may be the reason for starting the allotments but the exchange of ideas and help between the plot holders is a real feature of this community project.

The site was unlike any other, not tucked away in an awkward corner of town, but standing high above the River Dart, amid a sea of patchwork fields, with far-reaching views across to Dartmoor. My own gardening skills are limited but I am a great admirer of gardens, the order of vegetables and fruit, the random chaos of a wild flower meadow and the mix of colours in the herbaceous border – all images waiting to be captured by the inquisitive photographer.

I could not believe my luck, as here was a story worth telling right on my doorstep. "

Kim Sayer

Kim Sayer's photographs have appeared in numerous magazines including Country Living, Sunday Times *magazine and* Condé Nast Traveller. *He has travelled all over the world providing photographs for the* Eye Witness *travel guides, and interiors and architecture titles – and the still photographs for the many books that accompanied the legendary Keith Floyd's TV cookery series.*

Since moving to the West Country, Kim produced Part of the Scenery, *a retrospective book with Mary Wesley, and most recently an affectionate book about Dinky Toys of the 1950s.*

Kim's acknowledgements

Thank you to the allotment holders who, without exception, were always helpful and supportive and allowed me to photograph them and their plots throughout the seasons.

Thank you to the Simon & Schuster Illustrated team, in particular Francine Lawrence and Lorraine Jerram, who turned a pile of pictures into a credible book; and to editor Serena Dilnot for her expertise and designer Sally Bond for her stylish design.

Thanks to the writer Jo Monroe for making the story flow, and to Christine Walkden for her generous foreword.

Finally, thanks to Ted for opening the gate to the allotment field.